# 101
# WAYS TO BUILD A SUCCESSFUL NETWORK MARKETING BUSINESS

## ALSO BY ANDREW GRIFFITHS

# 101

## WAYS TO BUILD A SUCCESSFUL NETWORK MARKETING BUSINESS

**ANDREW GRIFFITHS
and WAYNE TOMS**

ALLEN&UNWIN

First published in 2008

Copyright © Andrew Griffiths and Wayne Toms 2008

Allen & Unwin
83 Alexander Street
Crows Nest NSW 2065
Australia
Phone:   (61 2) 8425 0100
Fax:     (61 2) 9906 2218
Email:   info@allenandunwin.com
Web:     www.allenandunwin.com

National Library of Australia
Cataloguing-in-Publication entry:

Griffiths, Andrew, 1966– .
   101 ways to build a successful network marketing business.

   ISBN 978 1 74114 959 3 (pbk.)

   Bibliography.
   Multilevel marketing. Marketing.
   Toms, Wayne.

658.872

Set in 12/14 pt Adobe Garamond by Midland Typesetters, Australia
Printed in Australia by McPherson's Printing Group

10 9 8 7 6 5 4 3 2 1

*To succeed, jump as quickly at opportunities*
*as you do at conclusions.*
Benjamin Franklin

# Contents

# Acknowledgments

**Andrew Griffiths**

It is hard to believe that this is the sixth book to be published in the *101 Ways* series, and my seventh book. I could never have guessed that this series would be so successful and there are many people to thank for its success.

Co-writing any book is challenging, but I want to say that writing this book with Wayne Toms was a delight (mainly because he did all the hard work). Having someone who is knowledgeable, flexible and diligent certainly helps the process but, best of all, working with Wayne is a lot of fun.

As always, none of this would be possible without the belief and support of the team at Allen & Unwin—who are in my opinion the best publishers in the world and, even more importantly, a group of people whom I respect and really enjoy working with. I also have a wonderful group of friends, business associates and family who offer me constant support and encouragement, which any writer will tell you is needed to get through the long nights tapping away on a keyboard. So thank you all.

And I have saved my biggest thank you for last: to Dr Debra Lawson, thank you for believing in me, supporting me, making me laugh out loud and often, and, most importantly, for loving me like no other. You are the brightest star in my universe.

**Wayne Toms**

Firstly, a very big thank you to Andrew Griffiths for giving me the opportunity to write this book with him. It has always been a dream of mine to write a book and to be given the chance to do so with someone like Andrew, with his experience, is something I will always be grateful for.

Secondly, they say behind every great man is a greater woman. I don't know about the great man bit but I sure know there is a greater woman. To my wife, Colleen, thank you for allowing me to fulfil my dream of writing a book and for also allowing me to foster my entrepreneurial spirit. Without you I would have never been able to realise my full potential, neither in business nor as a person.

Next are my family and friends, especially my three children, Rebecca, Melissa and Samuel, who are my inspiration and drive me to set an example so that they can see that dreams do come true, and that you can achieve whatever your mind can conceive. To my mum and dad for their love and support, and for their sacrifices in helping me chase my dreams, especially to my late mum, to whom I dedicate this book.

And lastly, to those in my office for making it such a great environment to be a part of, especially my PA, Katrina Neilson, to whom I am forever grateful and without whom I would be lost.

# Introduction

In simple terms, network marketing is a network of people who have access to a range of products and services that are distributed through that network.

Rather than operating via a shopfront, people can buy these products and services for personal use or to sell to others. Further to this, people can assist in expanding the network by inviting others to join the network, thus extending the concept to their sphere. Over time, and with more people introduced, the volume of products and services being distributed increases. Along the way, a portion of the profits on those products and services are paid to you and people in your 'down-line' (we'll explain some of this terminology later). In time, the opportunity to create a regular income from a team of people using and selling products becomes a reality.

Over the years, network marketing has attracted some less than favourable perceptions. The industry's image was tarnished in its early days of development, when there were no systems in place to educate those involved to go about their business in an ethical and professional manner. Additionally, there were many disreputable companies around who took the attitude of selling products at any cost, to anyone, with no long-term strategy; there were also some illegal pyramid schemes that entered the market disguised as network marketing companies.

Today there are well over 20 million people around the globe involved in network marketing, also known as multi-level marketing (MLM) or direct selling, and this figure is growing. Manufacturers, many of them Fortune 500 companies, now see it as a viable and credible alternative for distributing their products and services. Reaching consumers directly through traditional retailing methods and/or outlets is not only difficult, it is extremely costly. Today, almost everything—including health supplements, cosmetics, cleaning products, training materials, clothes, cars and travel—can be and is being sold through network marketing. Some of the most famous names in the network marketing industry include Avon, Usana, Melaleuca, Mary Kay, Quixtar, Herbalife, Amway, Tupperware, Juice Plus, Nu Skin and AIM.

Technology, especially the Internet, has had a dramatic impact on the industry, and more and more it is seen to be moving into the marketing mainstream. The industry is rapidly maturing and those becoming involved in network marketing are now more often than not coming from professional backgrounds.

Network marketing has certainly come of age. It is an excellent way to get into business, it has a lot of appealing aspects that cannot be found in mainstream businesses (we discuss this throughout the book), and many of the 20 million people involved are making a lot of money, for not a lot of work. They did the hard yards when they started but now they enjoy the fruits of their labour with a solid passive income stream and residual income.

Previously, many people saw network marketing as something you did on the side to make a little extra cash. This option is still available today, but for most people now involved in it, network marketing is an opportunity to establish a business that is, and will continue to be, their main source of income.

One of the biggest mistakes made by people becoming involved with network marketing is failing to treat it as a real business right from the start. Because there is normally a relatively low start-up cost, and a high degree of flexibility, some people treat it more as a hobby. That said, this concept does work for some people. They manage to set up a great little business which supplements their income and helps them to acquire the things they want out of life. But for many others, their lack of conviction ultimately results in the business slowly fading into the background—materials, books and products are left to gather dust on a shelf and the words 'network marketing simply isn't for me' are uttered whenever the concept is raised.

The main purpose of this book is to make you, the reader, aware of the similarities between building a network marketing business and building a traditional business. Even though the way each one works, and the end results, are different, many of the principles, fundamentals and attitudes behind making each business a success remain the same. If you can see your network marketing business as just that, a business, right from the start and give it the respect and focus required, and at the same time recognise that many of the principles and challenges are no different to starting up a pet shop, for example, then you are a long way towards achieving success.

Numerous network marketing companies are now established around the world. The way they do business, their structure and the terminology used varies from company to company. While our discussion has been kept as generic as possible, to encompass the industry overall, most observations are based on experiences with a particular network marketing company. If the references and examples we use don't always seem relevant to the particular network marketing company you are involved in, you can bet that the principle of treating it like a real business still applies.

## Why network marketing?

It is important to remember that you are *going into business* first and foremost; in this instance, the type of business you are considering is a network marketing business.

Network marketing businesses each have their own idiosyncrasies and opportunities. They can be incredibly rewarding on many levels and as challenging as any mainstream business.

## Working smarter, not harder

There was a time when simply working hard meant that you had the opportunity to get ahead of the average person who perhaps had a more relaxed approach to work. Today that is simply not the case. Although a strong work ethic will always be important, it is no longer the only ingredient.

Success is about being smarter and often doing things differently to the way we would have done them in the past. Network marketing allows you to do just that, while at the same time giving you the opportunity to associate with very successful people who understand this principle and who have made it work for them.

## Leverage and duplication

Leverage and duplication are simply the ability to leverage your time and to duplicate your efforts. If you are working in a traditional business, your income is largely governed by the number of hours you can physically work in a week. In network marketing, as your network grows, the time collectively invested within the network is dramatically increased, and your efforts are greatly duplicated and multiplied. Simply put, you yourself, one person, can continue to work 40 or 60 hours per week, or you can build a network where collectively, for example, 1000 people are working only 10 hours each per week, meaning your earning hours now total 10 000.

You need to understand that this concept is not unique to network marketing, but is a key ingredient in most successful entrepreneurial enterprises. Most successful entrepreneurs use it to build their wealth. For example, those who have established large franchising businesses base their success on duplication and leverage of one successful store, repeating it nationally and, ideally, globally.

## Passive income versus active income

Active income is best described as having to continually work, trading hours for dollars, in order to maintain that income. Passive income means that, in time, you don't have to physically do the work but you can still maintain the income.

Given the choice, most people would prefer passive income over active income. The majority of people think of passive income in terms of the royalties paid to recording artists and authors, or the returns on investment of property owners and shareholders. Further to these are the entrepreneurial business owners who derive large passive incomes from their businesses. In some cases passive income can be established without much effort; in other cases a certain amount of work may be required to maintain the flow of passive income. There are different models, but the concept is the same—do the work now to build a long-term income stream.

Passive income gives the recipients choice; they are not tied down to working hours for dollars but are in the unique position of having control over what it is they want to do with their time. Passive income provides the opportunity to have greater control of what you want to do in your day—if you want to play golf, you can play golf; if you want to do some work, do some work; if you want to go off on a holiday on a whim, then go. Passive income represents control, freedom and lifestyle.

Network marketing is a great opportunity to establish passive income. Many people who built successful network marketing businesses now enjoy the passive income they bring. To get to that point required effort and commitment, but the end result is worth it.

## Low capital investment

For many of those who dream of owning their own business, a major hurdle to be overcome is the costs and risks associated with buying an existing business or setting one up in the first place, often representing hundreds of thousands of dollars and a lot of risk. One of the attractive features of building a network marketing business is the low capital, or low entry cost, required to get started. The majority of network marketing companies require very little upfront money to join; what moneys are required cover start-up costs and some initial product purchase.

If a person goes on to successfully develop their network marketing business, the return on such a low initial capital investment can be significant.

## Low operating cost

The ongoing operating costs required in the majority of network marketing businesses are generally very low when compared with a traditional business producing similar turnover.

Costs often revolve around accessing educational and motivational material, acquiring business-building tools and attending seminars provided and organised as part of the support system. Further to this are incidental costs such as phone, fuel and other small home office operating costs.

As the volume produced throughout the network is built on the principle of leverage and duplication of a number of independent business owners collectively establishing their own businesses and subsequent volume, the costs in achieving that volume are greatly reduced by spreading them across each independent business owner. Therefore each business has low operating costs, minimising the need for staff, infrastructure and other normally high overheads.

## Part-time commitment still works

One of the major advantages of being involved in network marketing is the opportunity to establish it part-time alongside your current occupation or business. For those whose dream has been to own a business but who have feared taking the plunge due to the risk involved in giving up a secure job and income to delve into the unknown, this part-time aspect reduces that risk.

For those already running a traditional business who feel trapped and can't risk simply walking away from it, the opportunity to develop something on the side with a view that some day it will replace their current income stream is also very attractive.

After building the network marketing business part-time to a point that the income derived from it can safely replace that from the job or traditional business, one can then comfortably move into working the network marketing business full-time.

## Support systems

One of the reasons franchising has become so popular today is that people buying into a franchise do so with a sense of confidence from knowing there is a system in place and that they are not on their own. Network marketing also provides this sense of confidence—although you are in business *for* yourself, you're not in business *by* yourself.

Many network marketing companies, particularly the larger ones, have a substantial support system in place to assist the business owners. In some cases these support systems are run by some of the more successful business owners and leaders from within the network, people who understand the value of sharing their experience and knowledge in order to assist their own organisation grow quicker.

Another major benefit of having a support system in place is the opportunity it gives you to again further leverage your time—by directing people within your organisation to the support system and letting it do most of the work for you, rather than you being solely responsible for the training and support of those in your team.

## Creating positive cashflow

In their internationally bestselling book *Cashflow Quadrant*, Robert Kiyosaki and Sharon Lechter, strong advocates of network marketing (Kiyosaki is the author of a number of books on the subject), highlight the importance of creating positive cashflow if you want to achieve wealth. Most people operate in a negative cashflow—just look at the accumulated credit card debt. The majority of people run out of money before the end of each month, and 'when it's drastic, put it on plastic'. Most of them will spend their entire lives living from month to month, heavily in debt, and as a result will never go on to achieve their goals or dreams.

For the average person, once they find themselves in this position it is very difficult to turn it around, because the negative cash position makes it almost impossible to get ahead—unless, of course, they win the lottery that they are all waiting to win.

Positive income is basically the reverse, where your income exceeds living expenses. Network marketing gives a person the opportunity to establish a positive income by offering them a business that requires very little in the way of start-up and ongoing costs, something they can develop part-time with no threat to their current income and, in the big scheme of things, allows for very little or no risk.

More importantly, a network marketing business offers the potential of providing a passive and exponentially growing income that in time becomes a positive cashflow because the income outweighs the expenditure. Once you have a positive cashflow, that cash can be used to invest in other positive cashflow opportunities, and so on and so on.

## Creating wealth

Many people who have built a successful network marketing business have done so by recognising the possibilities in using it as a vehicle to create a large passive income and positive cashflow, and in using that cashflow to build their wealth.

For many, not only is it an opportunity to create a positive cashflow but it also gives them the ability to associate with people who themselves have created wealth and therefore to learn from their experience. Most successful network marketing business owners have found financial independence through their network marketing business, and many have used the positive cashflow to further build wealth through investments, property or the purchase of other business ventures.

# Reality versus fiction

Network marketing has become the victim of many misconceptions and some ill repute in years past. Sadly, in some cases a bad reputation was well deserved. Today, however, most network marketing organisations have to adhere to strict codes of conduct, their products have to be of the highest standards, and the high-pressure sales techniques employed in the past no longer work. Some of the misconceptions still commonly heard are covered in the following pages.

### 'It's a pyramid'

This is one of the most common misconceptions. Often when reference is made to network marketing the response will be: 'Oh, that's one of those pyramid things, isn't it?' Interestingly, when they are challenged, most people making the comment have no understanding of what constitutes a pyramid scheme, or even of how one works, and certainly have no understanding of network marketing.

Putting aside structural differences, the most important point of difference is that pyramid schemes are illegal and reputable network marketing companies are not. Many network marketing companies are now established in countries around the world where they have had to undergo strict government regulatory scrutiny before being allowed to open. Further to this, many network marketing businesses now deal with Fortune 500 companies, distributing these products or services through their networks, something the solicitors of those Fortune 500 companies would not allow if they were dealing with an illegal pyramid.

## 'You make money out of other people'

People often remark that being in a network marketing business is just making money out of friends or other people. But that's just what any business does—it makes money from providing a product or service to other people. If you were a tradesperson, for example, and your friends wanted to engage your services to have renovations done to their home, would you decline the offer because you didn't want to make money from them? Network marketing is no different from traditional business in that it has a particular product or service available for purchase by those who choose it.

## 'You will lose all your friends'

People involved in network marketing will often make many more friends as a result of their involvement. Because you meet so many new people while developing your network, and then work with many more as business associates over the life of your business, your circle of friends grows considerably, many of them remaining lifelong friends.

This is not to say that there are not people who have lost friends. There have been, and probably always will be, a minority involved in network marketing whose nature it is to be pushy, to not take no for an answer, to be very demanding, sometimes downright rude, even obnoxious. Usually these people are the ones that wanted to do it their way, and wouldn't listen to advice or plug into the training and support system. Needless to say, their involvement in network marketing is often short.

If you were running a traditional business and were constantly pressuring your friends to buy from you, it wouldn't take long to lose them—but as we know, most people owning a traditional business have many friends. Why? Because they go about their business in a professional manner. Your network marketing business is just that, a business. Go about your business in a professional manner and you will not lose friends, you will go on to make many more than you would have otherwise.

## 'It's a cult'

Quite often a lot of excitement, enthusiasm, motivation and commitment is displayed by those involved in network marketing. For people outside the industry this can be a little difficult to understand, and some of them can see the degree of enthusiasm as akin to a cult following—only because they don't relate to this level of motivation and commitment when compared to their own situation.

It is very common for people to slip into the drudgery of living a day-to-day existence, like being on a treadmill, experiencing very little excitement, enthusiasm, motivation or commitment. It is easy to understand why seeing people in network marketing displaying the opposite, being so passionate and committed, can be difficult to accept. More people are driven by an external influence, like satisfying their boss, paying off a bank overdraft or having a mortgage hanging over their head, than are driven by a personal dream or goal.

People who are attracted to network marketing see the business as an opportunity to get off the treadmill. As they begin to see results their attitude becomes even more positive, their excitement and commitment towards the business grows, and they are driven internally. People who can't grasp the concept of someone doing something without being forced to do so by an outside influence often come to the conclusion that someone must be convincing them to do it.

The whole environment of excitement, enthusiasm, motivation and commitment that surrounds the network marketing industry is often misunderstood. Probably the key here is perspective. When sporting fans go to a stadium with their hair dyed and faces painted in their favourite team's colours, wave flags, yell and scream alongside thousands of other people showing the same excitement, enthusiasm, motivation and commitment, we think that's normal. Yet when those in network marketing show enthusiasm and motivation towards their own business opportunity and their business team, for some reason it is seen as strange.

## 'Nobody ever makes money'

This is quite a common remark, and is usually the result of having come across people who've been involved in network marketing and, indeed, haven't made any money. If you haven't come across one of them yet, you will. There are, it is true, a large number of people who have not made any money from their network marketing business, and usually the first thing they blame is the business, not themselves. Most of them did not plug into the support system, were not teachable, did not listen, were not active enough in their business, did not give it long enough to work and, most importantly, did not treat it as a real business. If they had started a traditional business with the same lack of focus and respect, they would have failed there also. Because in most cases the start-up costs of a network marketing business are very low, this can be reflected in the commitment given to the business.

The important thing you need to know is that many thousands of people *have* made money from network marketing, much of it significant, and so can you if you decide to work at it. Being in network marketing is no different to being in traditional business—if you don't work the business, the business won't work for you.

The other thing that is important here is, once again, perspective. For example, how many people start a university degree and don't graduate? Good thing universities don't have a failure ceremony at the end of the year—if they did, no one would think that university works. How many people do you know who've started out on a fitness program, or joined a gym, and simply quit? What failed here: the fitness program, the gym or the individual? In business, more importantly, consider how many people start a traditional business and fail. The figures are truly alarming (in some areas, nine out of ten businesses fail within the first two years), and in most cases people lose everything as a result. If we focused on this fact, no one would want to start a business and the economy would probably collapse.

## The most important message

Being successful in any business is more about attitude than anything else. Sure, if your business concept is to sell ice to Eskimos, the best attitude in the world will probably not help you a great deal and in all likelihood the business will bomb. But the wonderful thing about most network marketing models and companies is that they have been proven to work in the past—which means, at least theoretically, that you can make it work as well. In other words, they are based on a tried, tested and proven model, not some pie-in-the-sky concept that could prove to be fundamentally flawed.

Throughout this book there is a lot of discussion about setting goals, having dreams, keeping motivated and having a positive attitude. We know that some people tend to close off a little when topics like this are raised, but we believe, absolutely and totally, that if you take the right mental approach to running any business your chances of success will be dramatically increased.

So if you take only one key message from this book it is this: approach your network marketing business with the right attitude, stay positive, have goals and dreams and you will make it work for you.

We suggest that you mark this page and read it whenever you have those moments of doubt or uncertainty (which you most certainly will have).

## How to get the most out of this book

All the books in the *101 Ways* series are written in a style that will appeal to the reader who likes to read a book from cover to cover, as well as to the reader who likes to open a book at any page in search of an idea or suggestion that can be implemented today.

*101 Ways to Build a Successful Network Marketing Business* is written both for those exploring the possibility of entering the industry, and for those already involved. It has been written to be as broad as possible, and is not so much about techniques as about principles. Anyone looking to start a business in network marketing will find it a valuable resource for years to come. Our main purpose is to remind you that you are in a business, and that many of the principles and universal laws of building a successful traditional business also apply in network marketing.

Keep this book handy and use it as a constant source of reference and inspiration. As you build your business, revise any sections that may be challenging you at the time. Use and review the 'Thirty ongoing checks and balances' section provided as a mechanism to confirm you are on track.

The other books in the *101 Ways* series will also help with running your business. For more information on the series please visit www.andrewgriffiths.com.au.

# 1 | Choosing your network marketing business

When contemplating entering any business it is important to do your homework, to determine the viability of that business and whether it is the right one for you. This first section covers a number of topics that you should consider as part of your decision-making process before becoming involved in network marketing. The message that shines through is that you can never do too much homework on any company that you are looking to work with. The more comfortable you feel with the company, the more commitment you will have and the more successful your business will be. If you are already involved, this section will also be valuable in reaffirming your decision or highlighting something that you had not taken into consideration previously.

#1    Finding the right network marketing business for you
#2    The good, the bad and the downright ugly
#3    Networking versus pyramid schemes
#4    Take your time and do your homework
#5    Always get your information from a credible source
#6    Anyone can succeed in network marketing
#7    Many fail, but many succeed in a big way
#8    There will always be hurdles to overcome

# #1 Finding the right network marketing business for you

For the majority of people, their introduction to network marketing has been through an invitation by someone already involved in a particular company, and therefore their only decision has been whether or not to get involved, rather than which company to get involved with. Today though, due to the growing positive exposure that network marketing is getting around the world, people are initiating contact through their own interest and desire to know more, and seeking out companies they would like to be affiliated with.

Network marketing and its acceptance is growing, with an increasing number of network marketing companies operating globally. Their business models, structures, cultures, products and remuneration can vary considerably; it is important to understand this variation rather than thinking of them as all the same.

For instance, you may have a background in the health industry or take a keen interest in your own health and well-being. A network marketing company that specialises in health or has a large product category in this industry may be best suited to you. It may be that your passion is for the beauty industry; again, a company that either specialises in or carries beauty products will be where you can take your passion and make a business of your own. For some it may be professional or specialised services, for others a company that offers a large cross-section of products and services. Other considerations could be that some network marketing companies suit your time availability better or that another's remuneration structure best suits your goals and dreams. It may be that you are looking for the security of a more established company, or the ground-floor opportunities that newly established companies provide.

Whatever the reason, with so much choice, it is important that you do your homework and find the company that's right for you.

## #2 The good, the bad and the downright ugly

In all industries there are the good companies and not so good companies, the reputable and not so reputable, the ethical and not so ethical. This applies equally to network marketing organisations, although, as we discussed in the introduction, the industry has come a long way in recent years, and corporate compliance regulations in most countries require and enforce the highest of ethics and standards. Most of today's network marketing companies sell quality products—if they didn't, they simply would not be able to remain in business.

What is really important is to make sure the company is credible. Due to the growing acceptance of network marketing, more and more network marketing companies are being established. The majority are legitimate but some others, recognising the trend, try to disguise themselves as a network marketing system when in fact they may be a pyramid scheme; still others are planning to be in the market for only a short time, make their money from the unsuspecting, and then disappear.

Remembering that the aim of building a successful network marketing business is to establish a long-term passive income, it is very important that you feel the company you are joining is going to be around for the long term. Even though the 'ground-floor opportunity' promoted by a newly established company is often attractive, much can be said for the company that has been around for a long time. Longevity within the network marketing industry is a sign of stability, credibility, a sound business model, proven systems and, most importantly, a commitment to the independent business owner's long-term profitability.

This is certainly not to suggest that newly formed network marketing companies are not legitimate, but to point out that those companies that have been established over the long term have the advantage of offering a sense of security and confidence to those thinking of affiliating with them, as compared to a new company with an unproven record.

So satisfy yourself; do your own research. Talk to other people who are involved, ring the head office or ideally visit it. Buy some of the products to satisfy yourself that they are high quality; in general, do whatever you can to be certain that this is an organisation you would like to be associated with. Don't believe everything you read, especially when it is online. Don't be pressured into joining any organisation. If you have any nagging doubts, listen to the little voice inside you. It will soon become fairly clear which network marketing businesses really are credible and can back up their offers and claims, and which ones to steer clear of—but in the end, it is entirely up to you and to your own due diligence and research.

## #3  Networking versus pyramid schemes

For the uninitiated there is a risk of unwittingly getting involved in a pyramid scheme, thinking it is network marketing. Unfortunately, because of the growth within the network marketing industry there will always be pyramid schemers around who will go out of their way to disguise themselves as a network marketing company. Due to a crackdown in recent times, these schemers are not as active as they once were, and the risk to the unsuspecting has been minimised.

There are many government organisations and watchdogs that can offer advice on pyramid schemes; a simple online search will give you the right organisation to contact in your country or state. Please take the time to do this.

Pyramid schemes are often extremely convincing and attractive, but they are unethical and illegal. Generally the person at the top of the pyramid makes a pile of money and the people at the bottom lose most of theirs. Pyramid schemers often target people they know who are in network marketing businesses simply because they already have a network they are selling to. Plus they are generally open-minded and they are motivated to get results.

If an opportunity looks too good to be true, it probably is. Network marketing businesses can make you a lot of money, but getting there takes time, energy and conviction. They are not an overnight path to fabulous fame and fortune, which is generally how pyramid schemes are sold to the unsuspecting.

# #4 Take your time and do your homework

When deciding whether to get involved in network marketing, or which company to be involved with, be sure that you give yourself enough time to make an informed decision. Be careful neither to make an off-the-cuff decision and jump straight in, nor to dismiss the opportunity without checking it out. Whether it takes you a week, a month or a year, take the time to properly research the opportunity. A word of warning, though: be careful that you are not simply procrastinating on getting started due to a fear of the unknown or because you are being influenced by the opinions of others.

It is important that you feel comfortable with your decision; don't be railroaded by someone 'selling you on the idea'. People who are railroaded rarely go on to build a success-ful business. A key to building any successful business is to be excited and passionate about what you do. With so many different network marketing companies now providing a vast array of different products and services, it is important that you find the one that is right for you, the one that you are excited about. When you are doing your homework, take the same approach that you'd use if you were looking to start a traditional business.

If you are looking to make a start in network marketing, use the following series of questions as a framework or reference point which you can come back to. Note down what you like about the opportunity being offered, and what you find challenging, and compare the results to assist you in your decision-making process. If you are already involved in the industry, still note down what you like and what you find challenging about what you are doing, and discuss your pointers with your support team.

## What do I like about the opportunity?

.......................................................................

.......................................................................

.......................................................................

.......................................................................

## What do I find challenging about the opportunity?

.......................................................................

.......................................................................

.......................................................................

.......................................................................

## What homework have I done?

.......................................................................

.......................................................................

.......................................................................

.......................................................................

## Do I have any nagging doubts that I would like answered?

.......................................................................

.......................................................................

.......................................................................

.......................................................................

.......................................................................

.......................................................................

## #5 Always get your information from a credible source

Far too often someone looking at a network marketing opportunity will seek the advice of people who are simply not qualified to give it. Nearly everyone has some opinion or other on network marketing, but when you challenge them, you will find that a large majority have no real knowledge of the industry or how it works. You must be very careful when researching your involvement and looking for more information that you seek it from someone who is qualified to provide it. The person who best fits this criteria is someone who has been successful in the industry.

When seeking information, ask yourself: Is this person qualified to be offering this information? Have they been successful in network marketing? Have they been successful in any of their endeavours? Are they entrepreneurial? Are they financially independent? Or are they struggling financially and going through life on a treadmill?

Some people will say that information or advice from someone who has been successful in network marketing must inevitably be biased. Others, the smart ones, will see it as commonsense. If you wanted to really lose weight, is it best to get advice on how to do that from someone who has tried and failed, or from someone who has been successful? If you wanted to establish a successful traditional business, would you seek the advice of someone who has failed, or someone who has been successful?

A word of warning on researching via the Internet. While the Internet is a great tool for accessing information, be aware that it also provides a platform for anyone to put unqualified information and negative comments on any subject, including network marketing. If you are using the Internet for research, do not let yourself be influenced by such comments without first being sure of the credibility of the source. The Internet can provide you with lots of valuable information, but at the same time it contains just as much valueless nonsense. You need to be sure that you can determine which is which.

In the end, you need to be certain that the decisions you make are not governed by information and advice given by unqualified people.

## #6  Anyone can succeed in network marketing

Two common questions are 'Can I do it?' and 'Am I the right type of person?'; the answers are 'Yes, you can' and 'Yes, you are'. That said, the journey in building a network marketing business is different for each person. Some already come with certain skills, experience and confidence that will make it easier for them, while others come with little in the way of skills, experience and confidence, which may create some challenges. What's important to understand is that both types of person can be successful, even though the journey and the time it takes will vary.

Take, for example, the story of two totally different couples who started in the same network marketing company. Anna and Adrian had professional backgrounds; both were well-educated and very successful in their chosen fields. They were well-respected, had a good network of family and friends and had credibility. Bob and Becca were from a lower socioeconomic background. They had only basic education and had struggled financially most of their lives. They had only a small network of family and friends and lacked credibility.

The two couples started their network marketing businesses around the same time. Each had their own reasons for getting involved. Each had dreams they wanted to achieve that their current situation could not deliver to them. Even though their backgrounds were vastly different, there were two things that made them equal—both had a dream, and both had a desire to learn whatever was needed to make a success of their business and achieve that dream.

Anna and Adrian's business grew quickly because the couple already had an awareness of success principles and the added advantage of credibility when talking to others about the opportunity. Bob and Becca's start was a lot slower due to not having been exposed to success principles before and their significant lack of credibility in the eyes of those they talked with.

Nonetheless, both couples went on to build very successful businesses, the only difference being the time each took to achieve that success.

Both couples have now been successfully running their network marketing businesses for a number of years and both have gone on to achieve the dreams that they aspired to. Do you think that Bob and Becca really believe it matters that it took them longer than Anna and Adrian? Maybe it did at the time, but now, after so many years of the lifestyle they enjoy, the time it took to get the job done has paled into insignificance.

Network marketing provides a great level playing field. Those involved may be tradespeople or professionals, educated or uneducated, shy or outgoing, but in the industry everyone is equal and everyone can succeed. What is most important is to understand that everything required to make a success of your network marketing business can be learnt, but the desire to learn is essential if you want your business to grow quickly.

# #7  Many fail, but many succeed in a big way

If you've never met anyone who has been in network marketing and failed, you simply need to get out more. There are countless numbers of people who have failed at network marketing, just as there are countless numbers of people who have failed at weight loss, a fitness program, learning a new musical instrument, learning a new language, finishing university or, more to the point, traditional business. Does this mean that no one can ever lose weight, get fit, learn to play a musical instrument, speak another language, get a university degree or have a successful business? Of course not.

The reality is that there will always be a percentage of failures in most endeavours but, as long as there is a percentage of success, it is proof that you too can succeed. The level of success and the time taken to achieve it varies from individual to individual, but if you have the drive, the motivation, the stickability and, most importantly, the dream, you can make it work.

So when it comes to choosing your network marketing business, once again we come to the key point of this section—make an informed decision based on all of the information at hand. Find out about the success stories, but also find out about the failures—and why they failed. Collect a complete and accurate view on the business opportunity to make sure it fits with you and where you are in your life.

## #8  There will always be hurdles to overcome

Network marketing provides a great business opportunity, but like all businesses it has its challenges and pitfalls. The scope of these, and their impact, will vary for each person, with some finding certain areas easier than others. Compared to some of the challenges and pitfalls faced every day by traditional business owners, those faced in network marketing pale into insignificance, but they are there, and it is important that you are aware of them. In particular, it is crucial that you are aware of the ones that relate to you so you can address or avoid them.

Some of the challenges and pitfalls you may face include:

- stepping out of your comfort zone
- negativity from friends and family
- people letting you down
- having to do extra work on top of what you are already doing
- not always achieving your goals
- giving up some leisure time in the short term
- extra strain on your finances in the short term
- frustration that it's not working for you as quickly as you would like.

Everyone who's gone on to build a successful network marketing business has had their own challenges to overcome and experienced some pitfalls along the way, but all of them have backed that up with hard work, commitment, persistence and a never-give-up attitude, something also required if you are to be successful in traditional business. For most, the road has not always been easy, but the trip has certainly been worth it. They will all tell you, 'Although it has been challenging at times, compared to what we were doing before network marketing, it has been easy.'

Don't fall for any razzle-dazzle. It takes time, energy and money to build any business. Go into it with this knowledge very clear in your mind.

## Notes on building a successful network marketing business

........................................................
........................................................
........................................................
........................................................
........................................................
........................................................
........................................................
........................................................
........................................................
........................................................
........................................................
........................................................
........................................................
........................................................
........................................................
........................................................
........................................................
........................................................
........................................................

*In any moment of decision, the best thing you can do is the right thing, the next best thing is the wrong thing, and the worst thing you can do is nothing.*

**Theodore Roosevelt**

# 2 | It is a business

When you become involved in network marketing it is important that you understand that it is a business, a point reiterated throughout this book. Many people in network marketing never quite grasp the correlation between owning a network marketing business and owning a traditional business. Even though the way each goes about doing business can be vastly different, the basic principle that network marketing is a business never changes.

To build any successful business requires an understanding of a number of basic principles followed up with commitment and good business practices. In this section we look at some topics that will set the foundations for you to go on and build a successful network marketing business.

#9 Treat it like a business, not a hobby
#10 Make a commitment and your chances of success will increase
#11 Understanding the universal laws of business
#12 Network marketing is a numbers game
#13 You may not like everything about your business
#14 It's not always convenient
#15 Manage your time, and profitability will come to you
#16 Having your door open for business
#17 Set up a separate bank account
#18 Manage your money wisely

# #9 Treat it like a business, not a hobby

An important aspect of this book is helping you understand that the elements of building and operating your network marketing business are no different to those of building and operating a traditional business. Most importantly, we aim to help you understand and reinforce that you are in a very real business, not just a hobby.

With this in mind, it is important that you treat your network marketing business as it deserves to be treated. A large number of people who undertake network marketing treat it like a bit of a hobby or something to dabble in, which is okay if you only want hobby results. Those who get involved for the bigger picture will be disappointed and frustrated if they don't approach it in a committed way or give it the respect it needs.

If you have become involved in network marketing in order to build a profitable business, then the first step towards achieving results is to make a conscious decision to treat your new enterprise as a real business—right from day one. Not having a shopfront or a factory or a big office takes away nothing from the business itself, and in fact is really smart, as overheads of that kind are what kill many businesses.

Your business has the potential to have a multimillion dollar turnover if that is what you wish, but that won't happen if you operate it with a hobby attitude. We talk about setting goals and dreams later in the book, where we make the point that you can build your network marketing business to give you exactly what it is you want out of life. Treat it as an opportunity that can be as big or as small as you want—but regardless of the size, treat it as a business and you will be well on the way to achieving your desired goals.

## #10 Make a commitment and your chances of success will increase

If you had just started your own traditional business it would be fair to assume that you would be devoting to it a considerable level of commitment, financially, physically and mentally. Understanding that your network marketing business is just that, a business, be sure that you devote the same level of commitment to it—not just to the network marketing company you are affiliated with or to the person who introduced you, although both are important, but to yourself and your business.

Far too often we see people who get involved in network marketing making the mistake of short-changing themselves when it comes to their level of commitment. The result is a sense of frustration that the business does not seem to be working, or is not working quickly enough, illustrated by the story of John and Jessica, who got involved in network marketing and were keen to get the job done as quickly as possible so that they could give up their jobs. Unfortunately, not long after they got started it became apparent that their commitment did not back up their goal. Soon John and Jessica began to make excuses about not being able to do the things that were suggested to them. They didn't attend business meetings and seminars, avoided the purchase of support tools and personal development materials, and weren't actively working their business consistently enough to achieve the desired result. Needless to say, this lack of commitment was reflected in the lack of success of their business, and their goal of giving up work as quickly as possible had to be put off.

Your business will require a certain amount of commitment from you in areas like time, effort and finance. Although these commitments are minimal compared to the requirements of a traditional business, they are there nonetheless. By making a commitment, you minimise dithering: 'Will I do this, will I do that, will I attend that meeting, that seminar, do I really want to go out tonight, can I afford this, can I afford that?' By making a commitment you have already answered the question and so you just do it.

## #11 Understanding the universal laws of business

If you are new to network marketing, have never been in business before, and you are finding some aspects challenging, ask yourself: 'Would this be any different if I were building a traditional business?' The answer, in most cases, will be 'no'.

In the operation of a business there are a number of universal laws that apply to most enterprises. Whether a business is large or small, some aspects never change—for example, cashflow, communication, establishing systems, marketing, time management, etc. Network marketing is a business, and some of these universal laws will apply simply because you are in business. One of the challenges often faced by those new to network marketing, especially those who have never been involved in their own business before, is the mistaken belief that these issues are unique to network marketing when they are first confronted with them. But if for this reason they choose to discontinue the business and move on to something else, they will find that the same issues still apply.

There was the case of Matthew, who had worked for someone else all his life but had always wanted a business of his own. On becoming aware of a network marketing opportunity he saw it as his chance, and decided to get involved. Soon he was confronted with some of the realities of running a business. Because Matthew had never been in business before, he thought that some of the challenges he was facing were specific to his network marketing business and soon bailed out, commenting that 'network marketing does not work because it's just too hard'. Some time later, Matthew started a traditional business, where he was soon confronted with the same challenges. Unfortunately, he found those challenges also 'too hard', and this business failed too.

To help you better understand business generally, buy some books, do some small business courses, and mix with other business people, not just network marketing people. The more you can learn about business in general, the greater your chances of success in your network marketing business.

## #12  Network marketing is a numbers game

The dream of all businesses is to have as many customers as possible buying their products or services, ideally 100 per cent of the total market. The reality is that all business owners recognise that they will only attract a certain amount of the market, or market share. In fact, larger organisations understand this principle so well that a large portion of their business planning is based around calculating how the numbers stack up. Based on experience and extensive research, most successful businesses know the percentages when it comes to market acceptance and market share. Whether it is a sole-trader bricklayer submitting a quote on a small retaining wall, or a multi-national engineering company submitting a tender on a major project, both understand that they are not going to win all quotes or tenders submitted. They realise it's a numbers game and that if they persist and keep submitting, they will win enough to be profitable.

Interestingly enough, the percentage conversion rate actually tells you a lot more. If you win every job you quote for, you are probably too cheap. If you get none, you are probably too expensive. The aim is to figure out what your conversion rate actually is. If you win five out of ten quotes and you want to build your business, submit more quotes. Simple as that.

As you build your network marketing business, for you the numbers game will mean finding those in the marketplace who may want to be involved and join your team, or those who wish to buy product from you. There will be those who do and those who don't. You can be sure of one thing, though—there will always be those that do. It simply means you have to persist, going through those that don't, to find the ones who do.

The bottom line is that doing business is a numbers game, and the more you work the numbers the better chance you have of winning the game. Your network marketing business is no different—not that you treat people like numbers, but if you can understand right from the word go that not everyone is going to want what you have to offer, even though you may think they should, this will make your journey so much easier. If you work the numbers, the numbers will work for you.

# #13 You may not like everything about your business

As exciting as the opportunity is, the reality is that you may not like everything about your business or some of the things you are required to do to make it work. In a perfect world this wouldn't be the case, but we need to remember that there are probably things we don't like doing in our current traditional business or job—but we continue to do them because we understand that they are the price we pay to achieve the end result.

There is an interesting phenomenon which we call 'business envy'. It's that 'thing' which makes everyone else's business look so much better than our own. They look easier to run and far more profitable, cause fewer headaches, attract heaps of customers, and so on. In reality, we have yet to come across any business that is easy. Business envy needs to be kept well and truly in check.

There will be times when certain aspects of building your business will challenge you and put you outside your comfort zone. There will be things you simply do not like doing, find uncomfortable or don't agree with. It is vitally important that as you build your network marketing business you recognise this fact: 'Yes, there are certain things that I don't like doing and find challenging—but this is no different to the dislikes and challenges I found in what I was doing prior to my involvement in network marketing. But the price to pay for the end result is insignificant compared to the price I had to pay previously.'

We recommend that when you are feeling flat about your business you take the time to write down the positive aspects that really do make it feel worthwhile—the flexibility, the freedom, the creativity and the satisfaction gained from getting results. Focus on these positives and the negatives will soon seem less overwhelming.

## #14  It's not always convenient

For most people getting started in network marketing, it provides the opportunity to develop a business part-time alongside their current work commitments. While this has its advantages, it also means fitting in something else around what could already be a very busy schedule. Getting started is not always going to be convenient and it may mean sacrificing some things in the short term. Things like a bit of TV, some of your social life or some of your time with the family may have to be replaced with time building your business. It is important to remember that these sacrifices are only short-term, and your reward will be to enjoy them full-time once your business is established.

There will be times when you don't feel like going to another meeting or attending a seminar or delivering product to a customer. The average person will justify this as 'not being convenient' and so will not do what needs to be done. At times like this you will need to remind yourself that failure is not convenient, that 'to do what others will not do leads to achieving what others will never achieve'.

That said, we strongly recommend that you enjoy the journey. Sure, sacrifices will be required to get your business off the ground, but take the time to enjoy the process, the thrill, the nerves, the anticipation and the satisfaction as the results start to show. This enjoyment will fuel you to overcome those feelings of flatness that everyone experiences from time to time. Ask any writer what gets them through the countless hours stuck behind a keyboard on a beautiful day when just about anything else has more appeal than typing another several thousand words; they will always say that seeing their book on a bookshop shelf makes it all totally worthwhile.

## #15 Manage your time, and profitability will come to you

Because building a network marketing business is usually done part-time alongside what is more than likely an already busy schedule of work and family commitments, it is important to practise good time management. This, of course, will be easier for people who are well-organised by nature than for those who struggle to remember just which day it is.

Whatever your style, one thing is certain—to make a success of your network marketing business you will have to be organised and manage your time as effectively as possible. We all have 168 hours in a week. Why do some people seem to achieve so much more in their 168 hours than others? Usually it is because they maximise their time by managing it better.

Fortunately, good time management is not a difficult thing to achieve. For the most part it is driven by being organised and working from a diary. If you don't have a diary or have never worked from one, now is the time to start. There are many great books available on time management to assist those who struggle in this area; for example, *Time Management from the Inside Out* by Julie Morgenstern and *The One Minute Manager* by Kenneth Blanchard and Spencer Johnson. If you are not the most organised person, we highly recommend that you learn more about time management.

If you are not into books, there are some great websites that offer online training courses in time management, for example, www.worldwidelearn.com and www.remotecourse.com. Or you might find that friends or business associates are willing to share their secrets and tips on how they manage to get so much done in a day. Time management is a skill that comes naturally to some but not to all. If your skills are lacking, do something about it.

## #16   Having your door open for business

If you were establishing a traditional business and opened your doors to customers only a couple of days a week or your hours were inconsistent, how successful would you expect that business to be? Having your doors open for business is presenting your business to others or selling some product, yet many people go about their network marketing business doing very little of either and then question why it isn't working for them. People who spend a lot of time thinking about the business or attending a lot of support training and seminars are often under the misapprehension that they are busy building the business, but in reality they are not keeping their doors open long enough to make their business work.

Here is a perfect real-life example of this attitude. David and Di, who were building a network marketing business, were meeting with Ian, their up-line coach, frustrated by their lack of results to date. They told Ian how excited they were about the opportunity and how they thought about it constantly, how they were reading and listening to as much support and motivational material as they could get their hands on, and were attending all the business meetings, seminars and functions that were being promoted to them. With all of this going on, in their minds they were busy building their business. But when Ian worked back through David and Di's diary over the last couple of months, they realised that the time they'd spent actually presenting the opportunity to others (building the business) was minimal, that the poor growth of their business was in direct relation to how often they'd had their doors open for business over that time. Once David and Di recognised the imbalance and addressed it, their business took off.

Taking time to think about and prepare plans for your business is important, and attending training and seminars is also a key ingredient, but if you want your business to grow quickly, do a regular reality check of your time to ensure that these elements are being equally matched by 'having your doors open for business'. You need to put out your 'NOW OPEN' sign every day to get customers walking in that door.

# #17  Set up a separate bank account

It is important to set up a separate bank account to operate your network marketing business. If you were running a traditional business you would not attempt to operate the banking for it out of your personal account; the same applies here. Even though in the early days it may seem your business is not big enough to warrant a separate bank account, you are laying the foundations of good business practice by starting off with a separate account straightaway.

Further to this, there will be expenses as you begin to build your business, many of them tax deductible. The costs associated with such expenses are far easier to monitor if the transactions are on a separate account. It can be difficult trying to identify them when they are mixed into your personal account.

All your network marketing expenses should be paid out of your business account, and any income derived should also be paid directly into that account. Don't make the mistake of paying any income from your network marketing business directly into your personal account while paying for expenses out of the business account, especially in the early days, otherwise it will seem that you are always spending money and never making any. Operating a separate account also allows for simpler accounting, which leads to easier assessment of income and expenses and the submitting of tax returns.

Another excellent reason for opening a separate bank account is simply that there is nothing quite as motivational as watching that account start to grow. As the balance increases, so does your energy and conviction. If the money coming in is somehow lost in the cracks there is little motivation to keep working on it. We play funny games in our minds, and a simple trick like this can have more impact than just about anything else.

## #18   Manage your money wisely

When operating any business it is critical to have in place some good accounting practices and a basic knowledge of book-keeping. You don't need to rush off and get a degree in accounting—that's what your accountant is for—but it is important that you respect the need to keep good records and be organised. In the beginning you may feel there is no real need to pay too much attention to this area, but remember, you are laying the foundations for a much larger business. More importantly, you are building a network of people who will look to you as an example and who will seek out advice on how to best build their businesses. If you do things correctly from the beginning, you will not have to go back and clean up the mess later.

It is often said in business that 'you can't manage if you can't measure'. Practising good accounting will allow you to better measure where your business is financially and thus allow you to better manage it. Additionally, the way you structure your business while building it can have an effect on its profitability; good accounting practices will allow you to identify problems a lot more quickly and act to solve them.

If you have never been in business before, make an appoint-ment with an accountant and get some advice on how to best set up your record keeping and books in general. Be aware that not all accountants will understand network marketing or be that positive towards it, largely because they've seen other clients not making a success of it.

If you are serious about your long-term network marketing career, you may want to sound out your accountant on their knowledge and support. If you feel he or she is lacking in these areas you might want to consider changing to one who is knowledgeable in the field, and supportive. Where a network marketing business is a supplementary source of income, and being run from home, there may be some considerable tax advantages and benefits, and possibly some pitfalls, that you need to be aware of. Getting the right advice will prove invaluable to maximise opportunity and to reduce risk.

Likewise, when you are starting to generate an income stream that is growing into a healthy monthly figure, you might want to consider how to best use this money. Some people use it as their annual holiday money, ensuring that they have a great overseas trip every year; others use it to fund a deposit on a new investment property every year. Then, of course, there are some who simply blow it, never taking full advantage of what the extra income could do for them and their future. What you do with the money you make from your network marketing business is entirely up to you, but we would recommend that you have some plans in place and ideally visit a good financial planner who can give you some professional advice along the way.

## Notes on building a successful network marketing business

..................................................................

..................................................................

..................................................................

..................................................................

..................................................................

..................................................................

..................................................................

..................................................................

..................................................................

..................................................................

..................................................................

..................................................................

..................................................................

..................................................................

..................................................................

..................................................................

..................................................................

..................................................................

..................................................................

*Even if you're on the right track, you'll get run over if you just sit there.*
**Will Rodgers**

# 3 | Understanding how your business works

Starting a new job or a new business always involves a certain amount of adjustment. There is a whole new culture to acclimatise to, new terminologies to understand and, of course, learning what your new role requires. Network marketing actually has more new things to understand than most forms of business, and it can be a little confusing. This section will provide a general overview of how network marketing businesses use terminology, how you make money from them, and their specific idiosyncrasies. While we can't address the specifics for every network marketing business in the world, we can provide enough of an overview to give you an educated understanding of the key points of a network marketing operation.

#19 Understanding the alphabet soup of your business
#20 What is the 'line of sponsorship' and why is it important?
#21 Compensation plans and bonus scales
#22 Rewards and recognition
#23 Ethics and conduct
#24 Get to know the company representatives

# #19 Understanding the alphabet soup of your business

Each industry uses specific terminology (jargon) to describe certain actions, roles and positions. Network marketing is no different, yet people often question the use of this terminology, feeling that it's somehow strange and difficult to adjust to. The result is that they get bogged down in the detail, and their business stalls before they even get started.

The first thing to recognise is that business terminologies are unique to particular businesses; your initial exposure to network marketing terminology is no different to starting a new job in any industry that you aren't familiar with. Recognising this makes it easier and quicker to understand and familiarise yourself with the terminology specific to the network marketing business you have chosen to participate in.

Much of the jargon used in the various network marketing companies worldwide is common to all of them; nearly all, however, have some specific terms. Terms such as *down-line*, *sponsoring*, *line of sponsorship*, *groups* and *front-line* are commonly used to describe structure within a network. Terms such as *diamond*, *emerald*, *platinum* and *director* may be used to indicate recognition of levels of achievement, or positions within a hierarchy; there may be other terms specific to your network marketing company.

The key is to understand what your company's particular terms are, what they mean to you in building your business, and to recognise they are simply a way of describing certain structures and positions within your network—this is no different to using terms such as *foreman*, *manager* or *CEO* to describe a position.

The key message here is: if you are unclear about what any new term means—ask. Don't ever feel embarrassed about asking what something means; in fact, it's crazy not to ask.

## #20 What is the 'line of sponsorship' and why is it important?

Within each of the network marketing companies there will be a term used to describe the connection between yourself, and those above and those below you. This is simply the lineage, or family tree, in a business sense, of those in your network. Although often referred to as a line of sponsorship, the term may be different in the company you are affiliated with.

As a business owner it is important that you familiarise yourself with your line of sponsorship and, more importantly, build relationships, particularly with those above you.

The people above you in your line of sponsorship provide access to a pool of knowledge, skills and information based on experience because they have been involved in the business longer than you have. In many cases they become your mentors, and are a great asset in assisting you in building a successful business.

Having a line of sponsorship also provides the opportunity to find someone you can confide in and relate to. The person who introduced you to the business may not necessarily be someone you relate to, or may not have been involved for very long and therefore cannot offer much in terms of experience. Using the line of sponsorship, you can seek out someone who can better help you.

A key to your business success will be both understanding and getting to know your line of sponsorship. Be sure you get to meet and build strong relationships with those above you who are recognised as leaders and are active in the business.

# #21  Compensation plans and bonus scales

All network marketing companies have some type of system to calculate and remunerate their business owners. Sometimes referred to as compensation plans, they are often tied to a bonus scale that rewards the business owner on the volume of products sold. The exact terminology used to describe the system of calculus varies from company to company, but what is vitally important is that you have a full understanding of your particular system and how it affects your business.

In some cases the way in which you structure your business, in terms of people in your network, can have a significant impact on your remuneration and profitability. In other cases particular products may be more profitable to promote and use within your network than others.

As a network marketing business owner, as for a traditional business owner, it is imperative that you are clear on what makes your business most profitable. Within network marketing, a key to achieving this is having knowledge and understanding of the company's compensation plan and bonus scale.

Many business owners within the network marketing business make the mistake of getting involved without having a proper understanding of the compensation plan, the scale of achievement required to meet the next level of remuneration, or the correct way to structure their business to make it most profitable, and so on. This means that they have no real owner-ship of their business, and just flounder along without having a realistic direction or plan to work to.

In some cases the compensation plan involves a very complicated mathematical calculation. The good news is that you don't necessarily need to have an in-depth understanding of the mathematics used, but you do need to know at what level you qualify for remuneration based on the compensation plan and bonus scale, and how best to achieve that level. In the early days of your business this can be difficult to get your head around, so sitting down with a company representative or, better still, one of the recognised leaders within your line of sponsorship, is strongly encouraged.

## #22 Rewards and recognition

One of the great features of network marketing is that many of the companies, and their support systems, focus heavily on rewarding and recognising achievement, whether large or small. It is often said of recognition that 'babies cry for it, and men will die for it'. Many people go through life receiving very little recognition; when they experience the high level of recognition given to those participating in network marketing, this alone can be a driving force to continue to achieve.

Many network marketing companies also offer non-cash incentives such as convention travel, cars and holidays as rewards for achievement. This again can be particularly rewarding for those who might never otherwise have had an opportunity to experience such things. Qualifying for rewards often gives the added bonus of being able to associate with the 'movers and shakers' within the organisation—and associating with success can only be beneficial. Also, as a leader within your own business you are setting an example by qualifying for such incentives. A great deal of respect can be gained from, and inspiration given to, the people within your organisation in this way.

If your network marketing company's support system provides such incentives and recognition, be sure you understand what you are required to do to qualify for them. Rewards and recognition can be very useful to you in goal-setting; more importantly, if it is something that excites others within your organisation it can be a great tool in helping them to set goals and achieve success themselves.

The concept of reward and recognition can equally be applied to people down your line. Remember to reward and recognise them whenever possible. The greatest of leaders and the best of motivators with a few well-directed words can change the course of history. This may sound a little melodramatic but it is true. Take the time to recognise and reward those around you who have helped you to achieve your dreams and they will only try harder and become even greater allies.

## #23 Ethics and conduct

Most network marketing companies, particularly the well-established ones, have some type of written rules of conduct, or guidelines that set out the role and responsibilities of both the company and yourself. As a business owner it is important that you familiarise yourself with them and always adhere to them. There should be no shades of grey.

Due to the previously tarnished image of network marketing driven by pushy, unscrupulous individuals only interested in short-term gain, anyone involved in network marketing today needs to play a role in changing that perception. Just a few weeks ago, sadly, an experience with a pushy network marketer aggressively berating us on the phone for not being interested in what he was selling reinforced the fact that there are still people out there who simply don't get it. That attitude has no place in today's world of network marketing.

You either are, or you are about to become, an advocate for the network marketing industry. We recommend strongly that you be ethical in all that you do, display unimpeachable behaviour and be totally professional. Through your professional approach you will develop a reputation for being a quality operator and will attract more customers and more people interested in being involved with you.

Further to this, it is important to make it clear to people in your down-line that you expect the same standards from them; ultimately, they can tarnish your reputation if they don't display the same high moral code.

## #24  Get to know the company representatives

The network company you are affiliated with will have inhouse staff and representatives responsible for certain operations within the organisation. A smart move on your part is to get to know and build relationships with some of these key people.

Remember, the large network marketing companies have not hundreds but thousands of people affiliated with them. In such large organisations it is hard to be noticed. Make a point of meeting those who work within the company any chance you get.

Good network marketing companies base their success on helping those in the network to become successful and having specific personnel available to work closely with you and assist where possible. Many of these people are passionate about their role, and take much joy in assisting others to achieve success. They are some of the unsung heroes within the network marketing industry. Having someone 'on the inside' can be of great assistance in dealing with the issues and challenges that arise as your network grows.

Spend time and energy in building relationships with those on the inside, but don't make it too one-sided. Be genuinely interested in the person and the relationship will have much more substance.

# Notes on building a successful network marketing business

.............................................................

.............................................................

.............................................................

.............................................................

.............................................................

.............................................................

.............................................................

.............................................................

.............................................................

.............................................................

.............................................................

.............................................................

.............................................................

.............................................................

.............................................................

.............................................................

.............................................................

.............................................................

*A man can succeed at almost anything for which he has unlimited enthusiasm.*

**Charles Schwab**

# 4 | Using dreams and goal-setting to succeed at network marketing

Within the network marketing industry you will find that a great deal of emphasis is placed on 'the dream', and rightly so. Dreams are the foundation of all success. Most accomplishments, whether personal, sporting, political or in business, start with a dream. Big or small, dreams are what motivate us to take action.

This section focuses on the importance of the dream, and the need to set goals to use as stepping stones on the journey to achieving that dream. This is a really good section to revisit on a regular basis, for the principles we offer here can be applied to virtually any part of your life, with amazing results.

#25 It all starts with a dream
#26 Do you need a little help to define your dream?
#27 The power of the written word to help you achieve
#28 Surround yourself with the right pictures
#29 Let your dreams evolve
#30 Go dream-building
#31 Review your dreams daily
#32 Be wary of the dream-stealers
#33 Set your goals
#34 Review your goals daily
#35 Goals in sand—dreams in concrete

# #25  It all starts with a dream

Ask a child if they have any dreams for the future, ask a teenager what they would do if time and money were no object; they will have no problems in sharing their dream with you and, more importantly, they believe it is possible. Everyone is born to dream and everyone has been given the ability to achieve their dream, yet as we get older and mature a bit, many of us lose sight of our dreams. Unfortunately, as we go along too many of us realise that our incomes do not match our dreams.

At this point there are only two things we can do—increase the income to match the dream, or reduce the dream to match the income. For most of us it is the latter, resigning ourselves to not achieving our dreams, or believing that 'one day I'll win the lottery/my ship will come in'.

For people who struggle financially for most of their lives, holding onto a dream becomes more and more difficult. Being involved in network marketing potentially opens the door to achieving your dream, but you can't achieve it if you don't know what it is or you've lost sight of it. Finding it difficult to dream is usually the result of a self-defence mechanism protecting you from getting hurt—'why think about something I can't get?'

Your dreams may not necessarily revolve around material-istic possessions; they can include things such as more time and what you would do with it, charitable work, being able to help family and friends, pursuing a sporting passion or hobby, even becoming a better person. People often make the mistake of thinking that a dream is simply something you want in a material sense, but that is just one aspect of what you might dream about.

The first and most important steps in making a success of your network marketing business require you to identify or rekindle your dreams and then to dare to go after them.

## #26  Do you need a little help to define your dream?

To be faced with a blank piece of paper and have to write down our dreams and aspirations is sometimes a little daunting. If we haven't really had any specific dreams for a while, pulling a list out of thin air can be challenging. But there is no doubt that if you want to achieve certain things in life, being very clear and very specific about your desires is the only surefire way to get what you want.

If you are struggling to define what it is you really want out of life, you may find these tips helpful:

- Divide your life into categories—business, family, health and wellbeing, financial, personal development, etc.—the number of categories is up to you. Rather than having one big life goal, work out the goals and dreams that fit each segment of your life.

- Quite often, figuring out what we want involves first determining what we *don't* want. For example, if you don't want to work 80 hours a week, your dream is to figure out exactly how many hours a week you do want to work.

- There are some great courses around to do with reclaiming our lives and clarifying our dreams. Ask around, talk to business groups, business coaches, etc.

- Read a book—again, there are many, many books on this topic. When you are working out your dreams, remember that they may change over time, that they are very personal, and that some are hard to define. Taking the quiet and conscious time to reflect and ponder the big questions is really an important step in developing your own dreams and goals.

- Talk to a close friend—talking about your dreams can really help to define them. It is important to have a high degree of trust in the person you are confiding in, so choose wisely.

Take the time to be clear on what your dreams and aspirations in life are. Once you know them, your chances of achieving them are greatly increased.

## #27  The power of the written word to help you achieve

Knowing your dream or dreams is the first step. The next step, and a crucial one, is to write them down, to make a list. There is much documented proof in support of the power of writing your dreams down rather than just having them locked away in your mind. A long-term study was done on a group of university students in which half were asked to write down their dreams, then add to them and review them regularly over their working lives. The other half were only asked what their dreams were at the time and not asked to write them down. Years later the results were astonishing. In the group that had written down and reviewed their dreams regularly, the vast majority had gone on to achieve a very large percentage of their dreams. The group that had not written down their dreams had achieved only a very small percentage.

When writing down your dreams it's helpful to break them down into three categories: What type of person would I like to BE? What type of things would I like to DO? What things would I like to HAVE? If you are a couple, each of you should write a personal list of dreams which are important and specific to yourself ('selfish'), then write a list that is important to you as a couple.

The reason for having a personal list is that parents (particularly mothers) instinctively put others before themselves and tend to list things that relate to a collective dream rather than dreams that are important to them personally. It's okay to have 'selfish' dreams as well as the dreams you have for your family and it's okay to achieve both, as long as one is not at the expense of the other.

Another tip is to break your dreams down into short-term, medium-term and long-term dreams. Think of them as small dreams, medium dreams and dreams that are way out there. Let yourself go, don't hold back, and always remember, what your mind can think and perceive, you can achieve.

Take a moment to kick-start your dreams list, under the following categories: 'The person I would like to be', 'The things I would like to do', and 'The things I would like to have'. Note down five things that are important to you in each section. Once you have done this, grab a sheet of paper and start to expand on each item. Continue to revise and build on your list. Don't forget—let yourself go, think of your dreams as though time and money were no object.

**The person I would like to be:**

1) ...........................................................................

2) ...........................................................................

3) ...........................................................................

4) ...........................................................................

5) ...........................................................................

**The things I would like to do:**

1) ...........................................................................

2) ...........................................................................

3) ...........................................................................

4) ...........................................................................

5) ...........................................................................

## The things I would like to have:

1) ................................................................

2) ................................................................

3) ................................................................

4) ................................................................

5) ................................................................

## #28 Surround yourself with the right pictures

Once you have identified your dreams and written them down, the next step is to surround yourself with reminders. If you have pictures or brochures about holidays, a car, whatever, place them in prominent positions where you get to see them on a regular basis. This could be on the fridge, the bathroom mirror or even on the back of your car's sun visor, so that every time you pull the visor down, there it is. There are even reports of some of the most successful people in the world hanging a picture of their dreams on the back of their toilet door! Surrounding yourself with reminders of your dreams is one of the keys to achieving them. Don't worry about what people may think or say—you need to know that this is something most successful people do, that it is a normal part of the success formula.

Successful people understand the need to surround themselves with their dream, immerse themselves in it and imagine they are already living it. Behind the success of many Olympic gold medallists are countless stories telling how they'd surrounded themselves with the vision of winning a gold medal long before it became a reality. One athlete had practically everything in her home either painted or wrapped in gold; whatever household item she could buy in gold to replace an existing one she did—bed sheets, towels, toothbrushes, soaps, hairbrushes, you name it. She even had a gold medal and its ribbon painted on her mirror so that every time she stood in front of the mirror she saw herself wearing the gold medal. She completely surrounded herself with her dream, and the result . . . a gold medal at the Olympics.

You don't have to go to this extreme, but the moral of the story remains—surround yourself with your dream and your chances of achieving it will increase dramatically.

## #29  Let your dreams evolve

Whatever your current dreams are, they may not necessarily be the limit of what you can achieve. Many people, as they grow older, find that the ability to dream is restricted because of financial and time constraints; your involvement in network marketing has potentially lifted those constraints and opened the door to achieving dreams beyond what you believe possible. Take this story for instance, of Gita and Graeme, who first saw the opportunity in a small group meeting being conducted in someone's home.

On that night Gita got really excited about the opportunity to generate extra income alongside their existing jobs. Her dream at that point was to earn enough money to buy the new washing machine and clothes dryer that they desperately needed. Once they decided to get involved, Gita and Graeme quickly went about what was needed to make the business work. In a relatively short time they were earning enough from their network marketing business to buy that washer and dryer. Once they'd got to that point they dared to dream a bit larger, and began to develop their dreams just a little, stepping up each time after achieving each dream along the way.

What started with a small dream has grown over the years to a point where Gita and Graeme are financially independent, own several luxury homes and vehicles, travel extensively, and own their own private plane. None of these things could they have seen or believed on that first night, but over time they have come to understand the importance of continually developing their dreams beyond their current financial and time constraints.

Knowing the importance of a dream and the effect it can have on our lives, it is important to be constantly developing our dreams and finding things that motivate us. Developing your dreams requires you to first, simply dare to dream, then go out and experience life and what it has to offer. Imagine, for a moment, if time and money were no object: what would you like to be, do or have?

## #30 Go dream-building

Nothing is more powerful than experiencing your dream first-hand. Having your dream written down is a key to achieving it, having brochures or visiting websites is important, but nothing can compare to physically seeing, touching and smelling your dream. Say one of your dreams is a new car—go out and look at the car, sit in it, smell it, take it for a test drive, so that you can experience it as if you already own it. If travel is your dream, go to a travel agency, sit with the agent and plan your holiday. Don't do these things just once, do them until the salesperson knows you as a regular. If your dream is to spend more time with the family, helping a charity, playing sport or being active in a particular hobby, try to spend a little time doing it and imagine doing a lot more of it.

Whatever your dream, be sure to find a way to experience it first-hand as often as you can. Make a point of going dream-building at least once a week and continue to do it for three months; you will be amazed at what a difference it will make in your life and you will never want to stop.

Going dream-building often leads to finding even more dreams. Building on your dreams is also important; when you achieve a dream don't stop there, but look to go on and achieve the next one.

## #31   Review your dreams daily

Once you have identified your dreams and written them down, don't make the mistake of putting your list away somewhere and forgetting all about it. An important part of the success formula is reviewing your dreams daily. At some point during the day, take a few minutes to review your list—have it in your diary, on your computer, on your bathroom mirror, anywhere that you can quickly review your dreams and remind yourself of why you are doing what you are doing.

It is just as easy in building a network marketing business as in building a traditional business to lose sight of what you are trying to achieve and the desired end result. If you don't regularly remind yourself of why you are doing what you are doing, you can quickly find yourself focusing on the day-to-day challenges rather than on the reward.

Your network marketing business is simply the vehicle you are using to achieve your dreams; your dreams are the fuel that drives that vehicle. Without refuelling that vehicle every day by reviewing your dreams, it can come to a grinding stop.

## #32   Be wary of the dream-stealers

One of the greatest threats to your success are the dream-stealers, the people who make remarks like 'What makes you think you could be successful at that?', 'Be realistic', 'Stop dreaming', or worse, make fun of you, laugh at you and put you down. Be warned, they are out there and they have a mission. That mission is to hold you back so that you don't go on to be successful and leave them behind or show them up as people who are not prepared to chase their own dreams.

Sadly, some of the biggest dream-stealers can be family and friends. Human nature is such that some people just don't want you to succeed or are fearful of change; sometimes, often subconsciously, they will try to hold you back. Witness the sorry tale of a young man called Jeremy, who had huge potential to be successful in network marketing. Jeremy was ambitious and had big dreams, he was motivated and teachable, and all these positives were backed up with a good work ethic. Peter, who introduced him to network marketing, believed in him and his potential. Unfortunately, Jeremy's circle of family and friends did not share that belief and were not supportive about his involvement. They continually put him down, told him to 'get real', asked him, 'What makes you think you can be successful?' They wore him down to the point he quit his network marketing business and went back to doing what he was doing previously, a dead-end job with no chance of advancement.

The world would not be where it is today if the people we admire and respect had listened to the dream-stealers. To be successful in network marketing, as in anything else, you must be aware of the dream-stealers and make sure they don't affect your journey to achieve your dreams.

# #33   Set your goals

The difference between dreams and goals is that a dream is the end result, while goals are the stepping stones on the way to achieving your dream. Goals are often fairly short term and activity based, just as if you were planning a long trip somewhere by road. You would have the destination as your dream and short-term goals for reaching certain stages along the way.

Having goals is the mechanism that keeps you focused on achieving your dream. They provide a plan and an objective. Without those goals you would wander aimlessly, without a purpose, just like two teams playing on a sporting field without goal posts. To be successful in any business requires good planning and goal-setting. Your network marketing business is just that, a business, and therefore requires the same tactic of setting goals if you want it to be a success.

Within network marketing, your goals may revolve around activities such as: how many new people you will add to your prospect list, how many people you will share the business opportunity with, how many sales you will make, and so on. They may also relate to results, for example: achieving a new level in the business, qualifying for a particular recognition, qualifying for an incentive trip, and so on. These are just a few examples. The goals you need to reach may vary, depending on the network marketing company you are affiliated with. However, one thing won't change, and that is the necessity of having goals if you are to make a success of your business.

When setting your goals be sure to make them realistic, measurable and achievable. Don't make the all-too-common mistake of setting your goals too high. Setting unrealistic goals leads to disappointment, which leads to inactivity, which ultimately leads to failure. Sit down with your coach for help in setting your goals; a coach should have a better understanding of what you can achieve. Be sure to write your goals down and a timeframe for achieving them.

If the concept of goal-setting is new to you, visit a bookstore. There are many excellent books that will not only reinforce the need for goal-setting but will also assist you in going about the process. Two that we highly recommend are *Motivation and Goal-Setting* by Jim Cairo and *Goals and Goal-Setting* by Larrie A. Rouillard.

## #34  Review your goals daily

As with your dreams, it is vital that you review your goals daily. Just as you would refer to a map on the way to a new destination to ensure you were on track, so must you refer to your goals to ensure you are on track to achieving your dreams.

Keep your written list of goals with you at all times. Use it to ask yourself, 'Is what I am doing now helping me achieve my dreams, and is it part of my goal?' If you are part of a couple, make sure to take some time out and review your goals together. Sit down with your coach and be honest about what you have or have not done towards achieving the next goal. Use your goals list as a yardstick to achieving your dreams. The more goals you set and achieve, the closer you are to reaching your dream. If you are not constantly reviewing your goals, the further away from your dream you will be.

# #35 Goals in sand—dreams in concrete

Even though your dreams may not change, the journey and the goals required along the way to get them may. Just as when travelling, you might have a fixed destination to get to but the route you take to get there might change along the way. Your dreams may be fixed in concrete and never change, but you must understand your goals are simply written in sand and can be changed if necessary. It is important that you be flexible, adjusting your goals when necessary if it means getting to your dreams sooner.

A good example of flexibility is demonstrated by Steve and Sandi, a young couple who had a dream of Sandi being able to give up full-time work and spend more time with their young family. They sat down with their coach, formulated a plan and set some goals on what they would need to do over a twelve-month period to make it happen. The plan entailed working with certain people in their business who they'd identified as looking to move on in the business, and helping them achieve their desired goals. It also entailed setting short-term goals which were the levels of business they needed to reach themselves at certain times over that twelve months.

As it turned out, not all the people who Steve and Sandi had initially identified as wanting to move on actually did, so the plan had to change to include others who'd not been identified previously. Not one of their original levels of achievement was met by the proposed date, so again their goals had to be reset—and they went on to achieve them. The end result, after fourteen months and much hard work and resetting of goals along the way, was that Steve and Sandi had built their business to a level where Sandi's income was replaced. They had realised their dream, and she could give up working full-time and spend more time with their children, and at the same time she was able to devote a part of her time to further building their business.

# Notes on building a successful network marketing business

..........................................................................

..........................................................................

..........................................................................

..........................................................................

..........................................................................

..........................................................................

..........................................................................

..........................................................................

..........................................................................

..........................................................................

..........................................................................

..........................................................................

..........................................................................

..........................................................................

..........................................................................

..........................................................................

..........................................................................

..........................................................................

..........................................................................

*If you don't have a dream, how can you have a dream come true?*

**Faye LaPointe**

# 5 | We all need training and we all need support

One of the great benefits of network marketing is that even though you are in business for yourself you are never in business *by* yourself. Very few people starting up a traditional business ever have the opportunity of working with someone who will help them get started and hold their hand in the early days. For most it is very much a case of learn as you go and trial and error, with very little training and support available. Network marketing, on the other hand, provides a great training and support mechanism which unfortunately is often not utilised enough.

This section provides an insight into the training and support systems and the benefits to be gained if you are smart enough to tap into them.

#36 Plug into the support system
#37 Increase your knowledge to increase your income
#38 Find yourself a proven coach
#39 Become a good student and be open to learning
#40 Systemise your business wherever you can
#41 Don't dilute the system
#42 Become duplicatable to increase your earning potential
#43 Use all the tools available

# #36   Plug into the support system

Most of the larger network marketing organisations have some type of ongoing training, support and personal development program in place. This program may be run by the network marketing company itself, or by a formalised support system organised by the individual business owners associated with it.

If there is a support system in place, the smartest move you can make is to plug into it as soon as possible. One of the many benefits of network marketing is the ability to tap into the resources provided by the years of experience and knowledge accumulated by those who have done what you are about to set out to do. Support systems give you access to this experience and knowledge, resulting in a steeper learning curve while you build your own business. As your own business grows and the number of people within it increases, you will find that you will no longer have the time to teach, support and advise everyone individually. When you understand the power of the support system, however, you will be able to plug your people into it and in so doing will successfully leverage your time and resources.

Support systems are in effect the university of network marketing. Just as we must attend a university to obtain a degree that enables us to practise a particular profession, so we must understand that if we wish to build a network marketing business and achieve financial independence we need to attend a 'university' to learn how to do it.

A very common mistake among people new to network marketing is not plugging into the support system, or deferring it for a while. They make this mistake because they already have a background in business and sales, or because they are already motivated. Not using the support system is a recipe for failure. If you were to look into the way people have built large network marketing organisations, you would find that they have all been very committed to the support systems and, more importantly, have been actively promoting it to others in their organisation.

If you want to build a successful network marketing business, plug into the support system available as soon as possible. Don't question its relevance to you, simply understand that it is a key element for your success and the success of those you introduce into your network.

## #37  Increase your knowledge to increase your income

Why does a nurse make more money than an orderly? Why does a doctor make more money than a nurse? Why does a surgeon make more money than a doctor? One person is no better than the other, so why does one do better financially than the other? The answer is knowledge. Each has at some point increased their knowledge, thus increasing their skills, and is rewarded accordingly.

Wherever you are financially at the moment is largely governed by the amount of knowledge and skills you hold. If your reason for getting involved in the network marketing industry is to increase your income, then it is only fair to assume that you are also going to have to raise your knowledge and skills, just the same as a nurse who wants to become a doctor.

The training, support and personal development systems available in network marketing provide the knowledge that gives you the skills necessary to build a successful network marketing business and increase your income. Just as we understand that a nurse cannot become a doctor without gaining the necessary knowledge, you too must understand that you cannot move up financially, simply because you want to, without gaining the necessary knowledge. Not understanding the importance of these systems and neglecting to plug into them will only hold you back. Just as in a traditional business, where you must gain the knowledge to successfully operate that business, so it is in a network marketing business.

There are many different ways to gain knowledge. You can self-educate, you can do courses, you can join business groups and you can research online. All are valuable and each has its own merits. Our advice is a combination of them all. Form educated opinions, increase your 'value' by increasing your level of knowledge.

## #38   Find yourself a proven coach

If you were to look at some of the most successful people involved in both sport and in business you would find that each of them relies heavily on a coach or mentor. Most of them, even though they've proved their success, will continue to utilise a coach or mentor on an ongoing basis right through their careers. One of the great benefits of network marketing is the ability to find a coach within your network who can assist you in building your business. Not only will they assist in helping you grow your business, they can be an invaluable asset in helping you grow personally and financially as well.

A coach will be someone above you in your direct line, someone who has a vested interest in your success. Be sure you find someone you can relate to, someone who has the runs on the board and walks the walk, not just talks the talk.

Understand that for a coach to give you the time required they will be looking for someone who is also walking the walk and is actively working their business. Just as the coach of a sporting team will devote more time and effort to someone who is committed, so will a business coach. Be open and honest with your coach, don't be afraid to share any challenges you may be facing. Remember your coach is there to help you get to where you want to go; they can't do that without first knowing where you are now. Be sure you tell your coach how things really are, rather than saying what you think they would like to hear. Also, having your coach assist you in setting your goals turns them into someone you become accountable to in achieving them.

Having access to a coach or mentor is a great asset in any business. In traditional business you may have to pay a lot of money for the privilege. In network marketing you have access to coaches and mentors who have achieved what you are wishing to achieve, a priceless resource, and yet it is available to you at no charge. Take advantage of this invaluable asset as soon as you can and be prepared to listen and learn.

## #39 Become a good student and be open to learning

When you start your network marketing business you will bring to it the skills, knowledge and experience which you've gained over the years. The scope of these skills and knowledge varies considerably from person to person, but one thing is certain—unless you have been involved in network marketing before, you will know nothing about how to build a successful network marketing business. With this in mind, it is vital that you be humble enough to put your ego aside and become a student of the business. To reiterate tip #36, a big mistake many people make when getting started is not plugging into the support system available because they feel their success at previous endeavours means they don't need it.

You are building a network of other people with their own independent businesses, people who will often look to you for guidance and advice. The quicker you become a good student and gain the necessary knowledge the quicker you will become a good teacher. This will lead to your business growing far more rapidly than it would otherwise.

Another important reason for becoming a good student of your business is that it is proven that knowledge equals confidence, confidence equals action, and action equals results. Without sufficient knowledge people will tend not to act because of a lack of confidence in what they're doing; when they do act their lack of knowledge tends to lead to a less than favourable result, which in turn leads to disappointment, which in turn leads to less activity. By becoming a student of the business, firstly you will gain the confidence required, and secondly you will see measurable results because your knowledge makes you far more effective. Become a sponge and soak up as much information as quickly as possible. Be prepared to listen to those who have the runs on the board and be humble enough to take advice and guidance.

Try to see your support system as your university course on how to build a successful network marketing business. Just as any student must attend a regular university to learn about his or her chosen career, so must you attend yours.

## #40 Systemise your business wherever you can

One of the great benefits of working in the franchising industry today lies in the systems they have developed to support their franchisees. When someone buys a franchise they are mainly paying for the right to buy into a proven system that works. Network marketing also provides this benefit. The support systems underlie a proven operation that has been perfected over many years. These systems give you the ability to build a large network by systemising the process and reducing the amount of time you would otherwise need to spend teaching and supporting the members of your network.

To gain the benefit of systemising your business you must firstly plug into the support system. The biggest mistake you can make is to have the attitude that says 'I will do it my way'. Thinking you have a better way than the system is a recipe for disaster. Once you instil into your network the feeling that it's okay to do things outside the guidelines provided by the system, they too will begin to do things 'their way' and before long you'll have a business that is not systemised, a network that is out of control, confused, lacks direction, is fragmented and achieves little.

Can you imagine what would happen to a company like McDonald's if they allowed their franchisees to 'do it their way'? The success of McDonald's is built on its systems; its biggest drawcard for people investing in a franchise is a proven system that works.

Understand that one of the great benefits of network marketing is the ability to buy into a proven system and to leverage that system into your own business and network. The quicker you can educate your network on the advantages of the system and the quicker you can systemise your business the quicker your business will grow and the quicker you will achieve your dreams.

## #41   Don't dilute the system

The support systems in network marketing companies are proven processes and procedures that have taken many years to perfect. In the early days of building your business you may not fully understand the power of these systems or why some of them are in place. The danger here comes when you decide to 'dilute' the system, promoting only those aspects to your team that you feel are important. There might be a new tool being released, a function being held or even a certain book or CD being promoted which you, because you don't recognise its importance, decide not to actively promote to your team. This is diluting the system.

There have been many cases of people diluting the system based simply on that individual's inability to relate to certain tools, functions, products or speakers. Understand also that your network will be made up of different types of people, not all of whom will relate to, or see the importance of, the things you see as important.

Another danger inherent in diluting the system is the impact it can have on your team's confidence in you as a leader. A good real-life example of this is that of Laurie, who decided not to promote to his down-line a new tool that had been promoted to him by his up-line because he didn't really relate to it or understand its value. A short time later, however, at a support system business seminar, this tool was being very heavily promoted and the results from others already using it were very plain to see. Obviously, Laurie's down-line questioned why they were not told of its existence. The end result was a feeling of distrust about 'what else we don't know or won't know'. This had serious consequences for leadership confidence within Laurie's organisation which took a long time to mend.

Your support system is specifically designed to cater for a large cross-section of people. By diluting it you are narrowing down the chance of others relating to people just like yourself. Just because you don't relate to a certain book, a certain speaker or a particular aspect of the system doesn't mean that no one does. If you want to build a large network marketing business, don't dilute the system; keep it pure and promote its virtues to all.

## #42 Become duplicatable to increase your earning potential

The great benefit of network marketing is being able to access a system that has been tried and tested over time and gives proven results. Building a successful network marketing business means building a network of people who themselves are developing their own business and all following the same proven system. In doing this, the growth of your business will be far greater than if everyone was left to their own devices. The biggest mistake you can make is to do things your way and not the way of the system. The risk here is that you can become so good at what you do that no one else can duplicate it. This will ultimately lead to you being the only one getting results. You will find that your business reaches a certain level that is totally reliant on you rather than the leveraged results of others in your team. By neglecting to follow the system you make it harder for others in your team to duplicate your results, which ultimately slows down the growth of the team and your business.

A good case in point is Rod, who decided that he would not utilise the system already in place for people to follow when presenting their opportunity to others. He thought it could be done better and 'more professionally'. Rod's background was in sales and marketing and he developed a presentation that was so slick that he was sponsoring a large number of people into his team. The only problem was that his presentation was so polished that no one else could do it as well, and as a result they could not sponsor anyone into their teams. After several months Rod found that his organisation was not growing because no one could duplicate what he did.

A key in developing a successful network marketing business is to be someone that others in your team can duplicate. Always remember, it is far more important to duplicate than innovate.

## #43   Use all the tools available

Your network marketing company's support system will have a range of tools to assist you in building your business. The type of tools available will vary from company to company, as will their affiliated support systems. The tools may include things such as audio CDs, books, DVDs and a range of brochures and sales support material. Developed over many years of trial and error, support tools are a great asset in building your business. As a business owner it is important that you familiarise yourself with what tools are available and how to use them. A tradesman understands that it is easier to get a job done if he has the right tools; the same applies to your business.

That same tradesman also understands that some invest-ment will be required to get the tools he needs if he wants to make a success of his business. You too will need to make an investment in the tools available. Don't make the mistake of trying to shortchange your business; all successful business owners know that you need to spend money to make money.

A great example of seeing your purchase of tools as an investment rather than a cost is that of Penny and Paul, a couple who were struggling financially when they started their network marketing business. In the early days, trying to find the money to buy the necessary tools was a real battle. Never-theless they persisted, knowing that if they wanted their business to work they needed to invest in the tools being promoted to them by their up-line. In their second year Penny and Paul reached a level in their business that meant a sizable income was coming in every month. More importantly, a one-off bonus that was awarded to them paid for virtually every tool, seminar and tank of fuel up until that point.

# Notes on building a successful network marketing business

..........................................................................

..........................................................................

..........................................................................

..........................................................................

..........................................................................

..........................................................................

..........................................................................

..........................................................................

..........................................................................

..........................................................................

..........................................................................

..........................................................................

..........................................................................

..........................................................................

..........................................................................

..........................................................................

..........................................................................

..........................................................................

..........................................................................

*When one door of happiness closes, another opens;*
*but often we look so long at the closed door*
*that we do not see the one that has been*
*opened for us.*
**Helen Keller**

# 6 | Develop yourself

Many people who are involved in network marketing will tell you, 'Even if I never make any money from my network marketing business, what I have gained in personal development alone has been worth it.' The network marketing environment, especially within the support systems, provides extraordinary benefits to those involved.

People who carry personal 'baggage' (in areas such as relationships, health, self-esteem and confidence) will find this can sometimes hold them back and adversely affect the business success they are striving to achieve.

For many people, too, being successful is not just about succeeding in business. More and more people are realising that true success comes from a more holistic approach, encompassing all aspects of their life.

This section covers a number of topics that will help you determine whether you have any baggage that might hold you back from your goal of building a successful network marketing business. Addressing these issues will also give you the opportunity to achieve holistic success.

#44 Moving out of your comfort zone
#45 Overcoming fears (and we all have them)
#46 The secret ingredient is motivation

## #44  Moving out of your comfort zone

Becoming involved in network marketing will require you to learn and do things you may not have done before. Like all things new, this will mean moving out of your comfort zone. This can be quite challenging, but it can mean the difference between success and failure. Indeed, to be successful in any endeavour requires moving out of your comfort zone—it's not just restricted to network marketing.

Quite often your personal growth and financial situation is in direct proportion to the 'size' of your comfort zone; your potential to grow both personally and financially is governed by your ability to constantly step outside that zone. By 'stepping out of your comfort zone' we simply mean doing things you feel uncomfortable with or find challenging. Once you have done them often enough they become comfortable, and you've created a new, enlarged comfort zone. Because your personal growth and finances are tied to this zone, every time you step outside it and create a new one you are also expanding your personal and financial potential.

If you find yourself having to step outside your comfort zone, get excited—it means you are growing personally and you are doing something that most people are not prepared to do. It is the sign of a winner. Although it's challenging, you need to understand that in doing it you are well on your way to achieving success.

## #45  Overcoming fears (and we all have them)

The single biggest thing holding people back from achieving their dreams would have to be fear. Fear can take many forms—including fear of the unknown, fear of what people think, fear of what action is required, fear of failure, and even fear of success. Unfortunately, we all suffer from some or all of these fears to some degree.

The good news is that feeling fearful is not limited to you—many of the people we look up to in all walks of life have at some stage had to confront their own fears before achieving success. Very few people have achieved success without having to overcome fear; the thing that unites them is that at some point they decided not to let their fears hold them back. Fear is the enemy of success. If you don't address it, it will control your life. The best defence against fear is action. Action cures fear. Have you ever noticed that when you take action and do what you fear anyway, the fear is often quickly dispersed: what we feared turns out to be not as bad as we thought it would be.

Some of the common fears confronted by people in network marketing are:

- fear of the phone (contacting people)
- fear of rejection
- fear of what people think
- fear of change
- fear of failure.

In most cases fear is perception-driven rather than fact-driven: or False Evidence Appearing Real. When action is taken regardless of the fear, the fear is often quickly diminished because we now see the reality rather than the perception. The challenge is that this can be easier said than done, but understand that if you want to achieve your dreams you must firstly be honest with yourself and identify what your fears are, and secondly take action anyway. Most people who achieve success are not extraordinary people, they are just ordinary people who've done extraordinary things. Deciding to take action in the face of their fear is one such extraordinary thing.

Don't let fear hold you back in building your network marketing business; understand that it is normal to have fear. It is taking action to overcome it that will set you apart from the average person who allows their fear to control them.

The first step in overcoming the problem is recognising and being honest with yourself about what your fears are. Use this section to note down the fears you feel are holding you back in your business. Once you have recognised them, sit down with your coach or support team and discuss each one openly.

**Fears that are holding me back:**

1) ...................................................................

2) ...................................................................

3) ...................................................................

4) ...................................................................

5) ...................................................................

# #46  The secret ingredient is motivation

The network marketing industry can be a very motivating environment, but for those new to the industry the level of motivation can be a little intimidating at first. A common mistake is believing that this high level of motivation is limited to network marketing. Anyone who has been involved in the corporate world or professional sport will tell you that having a strong motivating system is essential to success.

Within most of the network marketing companies and their associated support systems there will be a strong focus on motivational tools—CDs, tapes, seminars, conferences and rallies. The networks may also revolve around a strong recognition and award program. People who have never been in such an environment can have a sense of feeling overwhelmed, and sometimes are quite uncomfortable with it. This is normal; in time you will come to see the importance and understand the value of motivation.

We all need motivation. To do anything normally requires that we be motivated by something before we will act. Even the smallest task requires motivation to carry it out; getting out of our chair to get a drink from the fridge is initiated by the motivation of a cool refreshing drink to quench our thirst. More importantly, the more motivated we are the quicker we will be to act. There is even negative motivation. For example, if the average person were asked whether they would rather go to work or stay home today, the majority would respond by choosing to stay at home. If this is the case, why do they go to work? The reason is negative motivation. They are motivated by the mortgage, what the boss would say, keeping their job, paying the bills—none of which is very inspiring, but it's still motivation.

What is important in understanding the high level of motivation within network marketing is perspective. The level of motivation is no different to, and no less important than, what you would be exposed to at a weekly management meeting or sales reps' rev-up session within the corporate world, or in the locker rooms and training venues of professional sport. In all those cases the level of motivation is very high, but it's recognised as a key component if that corporation or that sporting team is to succeed.

The degree of motivation available within network marketing is a real asset. It may be a little foreign to you at first, but you will adjust to it quickly. Embrace it, take advantage of it and use it to grow your business. Don't make the common beginner's mistake of avoiding the motivation or thinking you are motivated enough yourself. Little motivation, little reason to act; high motivation, high activity. The greater the activity and the motivation driving it, the greater the success you will experience. Motivation is simply the fuel to drive your business forward. Given the choice, do you want two-stroke or jet fuel driving your business?

## #47  Dress for success

Your network marketing business is just that, a business, so be sure to represent your business in a professional manner by dressing appropriately. This does not mean you have to rush out and buy the best designer clothes and suits, but it does mean looking the part of a business owner. We all know the importance of first impressions; they can make or break you, particularly in business.

For the men—if you don't own a suit, simply get yourself a nice pair of trousers, a shirt and tie, and if possible add a matching sports jacket. You don't have to spend a fortune, but it will make a real difference to your business and to how you feel about yourself. Always make sure your shoes are clean and your clothes are fresh and pressed. Pay attention to your personal hygiene—be clean shaven or neatly trim your beard, comb your hair and ensure your breath is fresh.

For the women—dress appropriately and be conservative. When you're doing business you want the prospect to be focused on the product you're discussing, not on you. Try to avoid short skirts and revealing tops; wear appropriate business attire—knee-length skirts or long pants are best—and add a matching jacket. Be well-groomed but not over the top. It's not a fashion contest when you are working your business, but a contest of perceptions. You want to be able to give the impression that you are a professional business person who displays confidence and is going places. Always remember, perception is reality.

If you are a professional person with experience in business, the importance of good business dress will not be new to you, but many people who come into network marketing have never been educated in business dressing or needed to understand the importance of dressing for success. It is very important that you appreciate this aspect of your business; if it is a little foreign to you, get some advice. And don't worry about what some of your friends might say about you being 'all dressed up' if it's something they've not seen you do before. They might make some remarks in the early days but behind the scene they'll be secretly impressed that you have made the effort.

Your network marketing business has the potential to generate many hundreds of thousands of dollars in turnover, in some cases millions—are you dressing to match the potential of your business and give the impression of a professional business owner? What does the way you dress say to others about how you see your business?

# #48  Building relationships

If you are a couple building a network marketing business together, it is important that you learn to work as a team. Building a business together can be exciting and very rewarding, but it can also be challenging if you have never worked together before. If there are any relationship issues, now is the time to address them.

Not only is it vital to create a better relationship between you while building your business, but it's also important to have a good relationship once you have built your business and you have more time to spend together. Having a good relationship will make you far more effective and your business will grow quicker. As tip #56 explains, 'teamwork will make the dream work'.

An example which highlights the importance of a husband-and-wife working relationship is that of Mike and Melissa, who before getting involved in network marketing had never worked closely together. They had a good personal relationship but independent careers. After twelve months of actively building their network marketing business, Mike and Melissa were feeling frustrated by the lack of results. They organised to sit down with Jane, their up-line coach, to identify what was holding them back.

Jane quickly recognised that the problem was not so much what Mike and Melissa weren't doing but more how they were going about it. It became apparent that both of them had strong wills and liked to do things their own way. They were not really building their business as a team, for they quite often argued about how things should be done and where and how they should be working their business. The advice Jane gave them was simple: 'You need to get it together, together.' After recognising this and working on their relationship, Mike and Melissa's business took off.

Building better relationships is not just restricted to you and your partner; many people carry a lot of baggage from unresolved issues and bad relationships with family and friends. If this is the case with you, make a decision to start building better relationships with all those around you as soon as possible. It does not have to be an earth-shattering overnight change, but set a goal to start and build on them over time. You will end up feeling much better about yourself and life in general. There are many excellent books on relationships on the market; do yourself a favour, visit a bookstore and invest in this crucial element of the success formula on a regular basis.

## #49  Staying healthy and fit is good business

It is often said that it's no good being the richest person in the cemetery. It's no good achieving wealth if you're not well enough or, worse, not alive to enjoy it. Your involvement in network marketing has opened the door to potential wealth through a positive cashflow and residual income generated from your business. With this combination you can create a new lifestyle, which for many people means more time to do the things they enjoy doing. But it's no good getting to that point if you don't have the health or fitness to enjoy it.

Most people know whether their health and fitness levels are where they should be, and if they aren't, recognise they should do something about it. So why do so many people not do more to benefit their health? Very often it's because they have tried to make too many healthy changes too quickly (like working out too long at the gym while severely limiting calorie intake), and it all becomes too hard. Their efforts are often short-lived. To improve your state of health does not necessarily mean making radical changes straightaway, but it does require that you make a start and do something.

Improving your health and fitness does not mean you must immediately rush off to join a gym or dramatically change your eating habits if you are not the type to do so. It can be as simple as taking a walk every day and reducing the amount of not-so-healthy foods you may be eating. Over time, slowly increase the amount of exercise, and replace more bad foods with foods that are better for you. Health and fitness are often habit related, and if you change your habits slowly over time they are more likely to become part of your normal life. Try taking a long-term approach to your health and fitness improvement rather than attempting a quick fix. If need be, set a plan for the next twelve months rather than the next four weeks. Do a little each week, and increase it each month; over a year you will be amazed at the results, and it will be a lot less painful than trying to do it overnight. Even better, the results will be long-lasting because you have created better habits.

For most people, building their network marketing business means developing it alongside their current job, career or traditional business. Working on your fitness means fitting something else into what may already be a very hectic schedule. You may find this extra commitment difficult to undertake. But remember that improving your health and fitness will have the added benefits of giving you more energy and helping to reduce stress, which will in turn help you in building your business. You will feel better about yourself and have a more holistic approach to your life. More importantly, when you have built your business to a level that satisfies your lifestyle, you will have the health and fitness to really enjoy the time and money you have created for yourself.

## #50  Finding that elusive balance

Many people in traditional businesses today find the burden of it overwhelming. To build and run a successful business requires a lot of commitment and effort, and it is all too easy to fall into the trap where the business rules your life and you have little time for anything else. Network marketing has its share of people who allow themselves to fall into this trap. Your network marketing business is an exciting opportunity and one that can provide many benefits, both financially and personally, but it's not the only thing in your life.

Be sure as you build your business that you find a balance between building the business and spending time with family and friends as well as enjoying some recreational activities. By taking some time away from your business you will find when you return that you are more focused, productive and excited about it. Don't just get into a rut that has you constantly tied to your business.

As you are planning your schedule, allocate time away from your business, and make sure you take that time off. It doesn't have to be much, but ask yourself at the end of each month if you have done it. All too often you can get caught up in your business and it becomes all-encompassing; before you know it, months have slipped by and you have not taken time out to spend on other important aspects of your life. Balance is the key. Remember, you don't have to give up everything else to work your business; you only have to give your business all you've got when you are working it. If you want some more practical advice on trying to find or maintain balance between your business and life, *101 Ways to Have a Business and a Life* will push you in the right direction and provide you with 121 tips to win the war on balance.

# Notes on building a successful network marketing business

..........................................................................

..........................................................................

..........................................................................

..........................................................................

..........................................................................

..........................................................................

..........................................................................

..........................................................................

..........................................................................

..........................................................................

..........................................................................

..........................................................................

..........................................................................

..........................................................................

..........................................................................

..........................................................................

..........................................................................

..........................................................................

..........................................................................

*All our dreams can come true, if we have the courage to pursue them.*
**Walt Disney**

# 7 | It's a network of people

Building a network marketing business is building a network of people. Once they're in the network those people will buy and sell product. Without the people nothing happens. A large amount of the time you spend in your business will be taken up in working with these people to help them build their networks, which in turn will expand your network. Working closely with the people in your team, you will share their dreams and aspirations, their highs and lows, triumphs and failures, and along the way develop close and lifelong friendships. This section highlights the importance of network marketing as a people business, and explains what is required to develop a successful team.

#51 It's more about people than product
#52 Develop your people skills
#53 Understanding personalities (they are not all the same)
#54 Relating to other people
#55 Be the leader you want to be
#56 Teamwork makes the dream work
#57 Take your eyes off yourself
#58 Empowering people
#59 Lead by example
#60 Don't expect others to do what you're not prepared to do
#61 Have some fun
#62 People don't want a 'job'

## #51 It's more about people than product

Network marketing is, fundamentally, building a business with other people who want the opportunity to better themselves financially and achieve their dreams and goals. The people who get involved in network marketing do so because they see buying and promoting the product available through the network as a way of achieving those dreams and goals. The majority of the people who choose to join you will do so not because of the product but because of the opportunity to achieve their dreams. Once they understand that they can do this by simply buying the products available through the network and using them themselves, or selling them to others, then the product will move naturally.

One of your goals while building your business should be to know what the dreams and goals of the people in your team are and assisting them to achieve those goals. You do this by teaching them how to find other people who wish to participate for the same reason, then assisting them to find even more people; in turn you develop a larger network of people who are collectively purchasing a large volume of product.

The quote, 'if you build it, they will come', is very true of network marketing, with a twist: 'If you build *people*, the sale of product will come.' Always remember, your network marketing business is very much more about people than product; if you build the people, the volume of product will build by default.

## #52   Develop your people skills

As your network marketing business is very much a people business, it is imperative that you hone your people skills. This will come easily to some, but for others it may be a bit of a struggle. Either way it is important that you recognise the need to be continually developing your people skills, for you will be working and associating with the people in your network on a regular basis.

The first test of your people skills comes at the first meeting at which you present the idea to others. People will base their decision about getting involved not just on their acceptance of the idea, but also on their personal judgment of you. If your people skills are lacking you may not even get your business off the ground because of people, for whatever reason, not liking you or not relating to you.

Developing your people skills is not difficult. In most cases it is simply a matter of being humble enough to accept that you are not perfect and that you need to improve in some areas. Improvement usually involves the need to listen more rather than talking, and taking a genuine interest in people. When you are with someone, be there; when you are talking to someone, stay connected, don't let your thoughts wander.

Good people skills are an important part of building a successful network marketing business. Whether you are naturally good with people or not, it is important that you continually look to further develop and improve your people skills.

One of the greatest masters and advocates of learning to deal with people was Dale Carnegie, who was fundamental in establishing the movement that studied behaviour and motivation. His famous book, *How to Win Friends and Influence People*, is still considered the leading work for anyone wanting to improve their people skills. While it was written about seventy years ago, and the title may not sit that comfortably with us today, the pragmatic tips, suggestions and advice it contains are as relevant today as they were back then.

The better we understand human behaviour, the better we will understand ourselves and those we are endeavouring to work and interact with. Investing time, money and energy in this area of knowledge will pay off on every level.

## #53 Understanding personalities (they are not all the same)

Your network marketing team will be made up of people of various ages, occupations, backgrounds and personality types. To assist you in relating to people and improving your people skills, learn to recognise different personality types and how best to relate to each of them. One or two of the numerous books available on the different personality types would be valuable tools in building your network marketing business. We particularly recommend *Personality Plus* by Florence Littauer, and a book that is specific to the network marketing industry, *Sponsor with Style* by Robert A. Rohm.

Understanding the various personalities will also help you to better understand your spouse, partner, children and associates, and why they do the things they do—and, even more importantly, why *you* do the things you do and how that affects others around you. Identifying someone's personality type greatly increases your ability to relate and work with that person and can dramatically reduce the frustration that comes from dealing with someone whose personality is quite unlike your own.

In the numerous books on personalities, various names are given to describe the personality types, but fundamentally there are four types. There is the very organised person who is good at detail, the strong-willed and forward person, the bubbly and outgoing person, and the laidback and take-it-easy person. Some people may show traits of all four types, but are generally stronger in one of them. Learning to identify which you are dealing with will greatly increase your effectiveness in relating to them. For instance, if you are dealing with a highly organised person, always make sure you don't run late for appointments, and accept that you will have to spend much more time going through the finer details with them. The strong-willed and forward person will want to get straight to the point and attempt to control the conversation. The bubbly and outgoing person will not care for detail, in fact will tire of it quickly, and will be much more interested in what fun they can have. And the laidback and take-it-easy person, well, they will just go with flow.

A word of warning: identifying personality types is not about putting people into a pigeonhole and using that to explain why they do things and not expecting them to do anything different. Understanding personalities is a great tool to identify inherent strengths and weaknesses and to work on improving them. Numerous courses and programs have been designed to teach personality profiling and how to utilise it. Many people have spent a lifetime exploring personality, understanding it and defining different models. Understanding personality types can help us all to better interact with other people.

## #54  Relating to other people

The marketplace you are trying to expose your business to is diverse, made up of all kinds of people of various ages, with different interests. It is thus important that you try to relate to as many people as possible. To do so may require you making a few changes—changes like not smoking in front of people, not swearing, no excessive drinking, removing excessive facial jewellery, or changing unusual hair colour or clothes. This does not mean that you have to give any of these up, or change who you are. It just means that if you want to relate to as many people as you can when you are building your business, you may have to conform a little to what people generally expect from someone in business. When you are not building your business you can go back to doing what you please.

Trying to maintain a degree of individuality in terms of appearance and behaviour will unfortunately only get you so far in building a network marketing business; there will only be a limited number of people in the marketplace who relate to your individuality. Relinquishing some of that individuality will allow you access to more people who will relate to you better.

It is important that you understand that this does not mean that you must change who you are or what you do. It simply means that when you do business, you put on your business image and behaviour so that you portray a professional image.

## #55  Be the leader you want to be

A key element in building your network marketing business will be the leadership you display to others in your team. Building a network marketing business is building a network of people, many of whom will look to others for leadership. If possible, that leadership should come from you. If you can't provide it, that's okay, because one of the many benefits of network marketing is that leadership can be facilitated by someone else above you in your organisation.

Providing leadership can be natural to some, while others can find it intimidating. If you do find it intimidating, it may be worth your while working on overcoming your trepidation. Taking leadership over your team is very rewarding and provides a greater sense of ownership. It can also mean quicker growth and results for your business. Also remember that leadership is taken, not given; when you start out there will more than likely be someone above you leading the organisation who will continue to do so until you take leadership of your team. That does not mean a leadership coup, but a natural transfer of leadership from that person to you as you take greater ownership and responsibility in a mutually beneficial transition.

An interesting exercise is to think about a boss you've had in the past who you really liked. What was it about this person and their leadership style that you admired? How did you feel when you worked with them and what motivated you? Then think about a boss you didn't like, and ask yourself what it was that you really disliked, and how you felt when you worked for them. Reflecting on the good boss often defines your views on being a leader and how you want to be seen, while the bad boss defines the characteristics that you don't want (obviously enough).

The moral to the story here is to be the leader you really want to be. Think of yourself as that leader, with their own style, values and qualities, and ultimately that is the leader you will become.

## #56  Teamwork makes the dream work

Your success in network marketing is very much based on how many others within your team you have helped on their way to success. Real success in network marketing is fundamentally a team effort. Many of the large network marketing organisations around the world owe their success to the great team spirit they have been able to instil among their people.

People like to be part of a winning team. By lifting the team spirit and getting everyone behind the success of others in your team you can create a frenzy of enthusiasm and excitement. Network marketing creates strong friendships and an even greater sense of team involvement if nurtured properly. Being an individual will only get you so far; you may experience a certain amount of success, but your ability to build a large organisation will be greatly impeded.

People love to be a part of something bigger than themselves, they love to share in the excitement of others' success. Never forget that you are building a team—it is the team, not you alone, that will mean the difference in achieving your dreams and goals.

## #57  Take your eyes off yourself

The cornerstone of success in network marketing is the principle that success in achieving your goals and dreams is only reached when you help others in your team achieve their goals and dreams. With this in mind, the quickest way for you to get what you want is to find as many people as possible who also have goals and dreams, then take your eyes off yourself and onto your people and help them achieve their goals.

A good example of this comes from Rick and Rowena, who were suffering desperate financial difficulties at the time that they were introduced to network marketing. They could see that it could be the answer to their prayers, but to get themselves out of the situation they were in they would have to build a very large organisation quickly. Having a good understanding of how the business worked, Rick and Rowena set about finding half a dozen other couples who had small, short-term goals. If they could help these people achieve these goals they, by default, would achieve theirs. With this in mind they simply took their eyes off themselves and worked with the other couples, over a short time helping each achieve their goals. Not only did Rick and Rowena find it extremely rewarding to have helped these couples, it also resulted in their building a large organisation, with the result that they turned around their financial situation totally.

Be aware that many people find this 'helping others' hard to get their heads around initially because, unfortunately, in today's world it has very much become a case of others taking advantage of you rather than helping you. It can be difficult in the early days of your business to understand why someone would be prepared to spend so much time and effort and, in many cases, money, to help you succeed. Many people are at first suspicious and waiting for the 'catch'; it can be difficult to grasp the concept of a win-win situation whereby you helping them become successful will help to make you successful.

Network marketing is a great concept in terms of this 'take your eyes off yourself and help others' philosophy. Those who come into the industry without this philosophy, the people who try to use others to achieve their end result, only last a short time. The system quickly filters them out.

## #58 Empowering people

There will be people in your team who will lack confidence and self-esteem. These people will require extra attention from you, needing to be continually reminded that they can do it and that you believe in them. Many of them will have spent their entire lives being told they won't amount to anything, can't be successful, or believing they are failures. Their involvement in network marketing means that they are not failures; they can succeed, but they are going to have to be reminded of that constantly to erase the old programming.

Many of those who fail in network marketing (apart from the self-centred type discussed earlier) have come into the industry carrying this emotional baggage, and unfortunately don't stay long enough to remedy the negative programming. If you are one of them, make a decision right here, right now, that you are not going to let the influence of others rule your life.

If you find people in your team who suffer from a lack of confidence or low self-esteem, you must do your very best to empower them with your genuine belief in them; assure them that you will stand by them and make it happen. Even though they need to hear it more often than others, be conscious that everyone in your team will need to hear it every now and then. Telling someone that you believe in them, that you believe they can do it, is never a waste of time. Many successful network marketing businesses are built on the belief of others. Empowerment is one of the greatest gifts you can give another person; the network marketing environment is a great place for putting empowerment to good use.

## #59 Lead by example

The best way to build your business quickly is to lead by example. Don't fall into the trap of promoting how good the opportunity is or how good the products are if you are not currently active in the business or not using the products yourself. If the network marketing company you are affiliated with, or its support system, has business building tools available like books, CDs or seminars that help to grow the business, don't promote their use if you are not prepared to practise what you preach.

The people in your team, particularly the new ones, are looking to you as an example—make sure that you are setting it. If promotions or incentives are being offered by the network marketing company, make sure that you are the one setting the pace and leading from the front. If your organisation has a recognition program, make sure that your team sees you being recognised and moving ahead. Leading by example sends the message that you are serious. It also instils confidence in your team that it works. Your team will become inspired, and this will result in rapid growth. People love to be part of a winning team.

## #60  Don't expect others to do what you're not prepared to do

When you are coaching or teaching people within your team on various aspects of building their network marketing business, make certain you are not telling them to do something which you are not prepared to do yourself. It can be easy to fall into this trap because it often seems easier to have others do it rather than doing it yourself, but this is a very dangerous place to be. For example, don't advise and expect people to do things such as looking for new prospects, showing the opportunity to others or selling products if, for whatever reason, you are not willing to do it yourself.

The very best teaching is by example. People will learn so much more from you leading by example than from any theory. Although advice is important, advising someone on how to do something can never compete with showing how it's done. Further to this is the danger of losing touch with what really needs to be done because it's been so long since you've done it yourself, which often leads to giving the wrong advice.

If someone asks you for advice on a certain aspect of building the business that you are struggling with yourself, refer them on to someone who has a better understanding of what needs to be done. More importantly, don't promote to others what it takes to build a successful network marketing business if you are not prepared to go out and do it yourself.

## #61   Have some fun

As you develop your team and it begins to grow in size, it can be all too easy to get so busy and so focused that you forget to stop to smell the roses and have some fun. Not only that, but the people around you, in your team and in your family, will soon grow tired of being in a very rigid and businesslike environment all the time. People like to have a good time and have some fun. Network marketing is a very positive and uplifting environment. Taking some time out and having fun fits in well.

As part of building your business, plan regular social get-togethers with your team. Do something out of the ordinary, like fancy dress parties or trivia nights. Organise barbecues with them and their families, dinner parties, weekends away, karaoke, anything at all; just make sure that you are doing something on a regular basis that involves your team and having some fun.

Another idea is to run a special promotion in your team from time to time, setting some activity or achievement goal where those who qualify get to attend a special event you are organising. This could include time with a well-respected leader in your up-line who has offered their time to support you.

A story that highlights the benefits of organising such events is that of Jim and Jacqui. Both came into network marketing after long careers in a very rigid and stuffy corporate world. During their respective careers there was no time for fun and their lives were very fast-paced. Unfortunately, they carried over these old work habits into their network marketing business and, even though they achieved success in developing a sizable team, it was not long before the team started to become stale and disheartened by the 'all work and no play' environment. Recognising the problem, their up-line coach suggested a promotion for members of the team. All of the qualifiers would be able to attend a 'family fun weekend' away. No business was to be discussed over the weekend and a range of fun activities with like-minded people was organised. The weekend also included the opportunity to spend time on a social level with a well-respected leader and his family.

The results of the promotion were amazing: Jim and Jacqui experienced huge growth in their business volume and saw their team re-energised. Since then Jim and Jacqui have run frequent similar promotions and other fun events on a regular basis, and both agree that it has been a very important element in their ongoing success.

The moral of this tip is simple—having fun is good for business. We enjoy doing business with people we like and just about everyone enjoys having fun! So incorporate as much as you can into your daily life and never make the mistake of thinking that having fun is unprofessional.

## #62 People don't want a 'job'

One of the things that attracts people to network marketing is the prospect of having a business of their own, of getting away from a boss telling them what to do. As you build your team, always remember that it is made up of individual business owners, and the last thing they want from you as their leader is being told what to do. Because they are joining you to get away from a 'job', and looking to feel a sense of ownership and to be part of a team, you must be careful you don't fall into the trap of treating them as subordinates so that they see you as another boss.

Your role is to lead and empower those in your team, not to boss them. You have to ensure that they have a sense of involvement in the team, that they maintain ownership of their own business. Becoming a mentor or coach to your team is different to bossing them. As mentor and coach you advise and counsel your people, but leave it up to them to make the final decision on what they should do.

# Notes on building a successful network marketing business

...................................................................
...................................................................
...................................................................
...................................................................
...................................................................
...................................................................
...................................................................
...................................................................
...................................................................
...................................................................
...................................................................
...................................................................
...................................................................
...................................................................
...................................................................
...................................................................
...................................................................
...................................................................
...................................................................
...................................................................

*Keep away from people who try to belittle your ambition. Small people always do that, but the really great make you feel that you, too, can become great.*

Mark Twain

# 8 | Products and selling

If your dream has been to own your own business, some type of product or service has to be sold through that business if it is to make a profit. This section focuses on the area of products and selling within network marketing and the importance of making the most of this aspect of your business. More importantly, it reinforces the message that network marketing is also a business and as a result selling will be involved.

#63 Know your products thoroughly
#64 Be a 100% user of your own products
#65 Pay for the products you use yourself
#66 Selling is part of any business
#67 A little multiplied by many equals a lot
#68 Using retail profit to help build your business

## #63   Know your products thoroughly

It is imperative that any business owner has a good knowledge and understanding of the products or services which that business supplies. Being in network marketing is no different, yet many people involved in the industry have far too little understanding and knowledge of the products available through the company they are affiliated with. To make a success of your network marketing business you must firstly make yourself aware of what products are available, and secondly educate yourself on their use. Most network marketing companies, the good ones, have a strong resource department to support product knowledge. This can be in the form of literature, CDs, DVDs and product training seminars. The danger in not having this product knowledge is the threat to your perceived credibility among those you are looking to bring into your team and those already a part of it. Understandably, if they question you on one of the products or services available through the network and you know nothing about it, this will affect your credibility. The same applies to a customer you are trying to sell your products to. Can you imagine how you would feel if you walked into a retail store and no one had any idea about the product or service you were interested in buying? Would you deal with them again in the future?

As a business owner it is important that you know the key features and benefits of your products for your customers, and the advantages they have over any similar products on the market. You must believe in the quality and value of your product if you are to inspire others to join you in your business and sell them to customers.

# #64   Be a 100% user of your own products

If you were a butcher who owned your own business, you would not go down the street to buy your meat from someone else. More importantly, you would not want your customers to see you doing it. If you owned a takeaway food shop, you would not go next door to buy your takeaway, and nor would you want your customers seeing you go next door. Both examples would send the message to others that you didn't believe in your business or its product. The end result would be business suicide.

If what is available to you through your network marketing company is products or services you normally use, you must always buy them from yourself and not from a competitor down the road. Building a successful network marketing business is about building a team of people who are duplicating you. If you are not using your own products, the people in your network will see this as a message that you don't really believe in what you are doing. They will copy your message and not buy product themselves. It will only take them seeing you use just one product from a competitor, even when you are using all your own products as well, to plant a seed of doubt.

The number of products available through each of the various network marketing companies varies considerably. Some have a very limited, sometimes specific, range of products, while others' product lines are very diverse, almost a grocery store range. Whatever the range available to you through the company you are affiliated with, if it includes product you would normally purchase, be sure to buy it through your own business.

## #65  Pay for the products you use yourself

If an item you need is available in a store down the road, you would never go into that store, pick it off the shelf and walk out without paying. Yet many people operating a network marketing business will order a product which they require for personal use through their business without paying their business for it. This is the same as walking out without paying.

When buying products through your network marketing company for personal use, always pay for them out of your personal account. This may seem like commonsense, but you would be surprised how many people order and pay for personal-use product out of their business account, and don't reimburse that account. The end result is a business account that never reconciles, that always seems to have more money going out than in, which fosters the negative attitude that 'my business doesn't make any money'.

In most network marketing companies your business will purchase products at wholesale price and sell at retail price. When paying for products for personal use, instead of just reimbursing your business the wholesale price you could elect to pay the retail price, as you would have done if you'd bought that product from the store down the street. The result is added profit going into your business that you can use to further build your business.

## #66  Selling is part of any business

To be in business, any business, always involves the need to sell. The level of selling required depends on the type of business, but you can be sure that selling will be involved. Being in business is not just about selling products or services; in many cases it's also about selling yourself and your business. People looking to build a network marketing business will sometimes come up with objections such as, 'But I don't like to sell' or 'I don't see myself as a salesperson' or 'I don't have the gift of the gab'. If this is the sole reason for deciding not to get into, or not continuing to build, your network marketing business, then the unfortunate reality is that having your own business, any business, may not be for you.

Depending on the network marketing company you are associated with, the type and amount of selling required will vary. In most cases you will need to sell products, and sell the business concept to others. In some network marketing company business models, the business is very much driven by business owners selling products to retail customers, while others are based around building volume through your own personal use and the personal use of others within a network, combined with a small amount of retail selling.

## #67 A little multiplied by many equals a lot

One of the great benefits of building a network marketing business is the ability it gives you to leverage your efforts. For those who find the selling of products a bit of a challenge, the good news is you don't have to do that much compared to what you would have to do in a traditional business. Even if you can learn to sell a little and teach others to do the same, the little you do multiplied by others within your network doing the same equals a lot; in fact, it can equal many tens of thousands of dollars in volume. Would you prefer to go out and sell tens of thousands of dollars worth of products yourself, or sell only a small percentage of that volume and leverage yourself to get the same result?

It is also important to understand that leverage within network marketing is achieved through others within your business duplicating you. In other words, unless you can learn to move even just a small amount of product through selling, the chances are that you are not going to be able to teach others to do it, and you won't achieve the advantages of leverage. A duplication of yourself selling no product can ultimately lead to nothing; nothing multiplied by many still equals nothing! Needless to say, the more products you can sell, the better chance there is of others duplicating what you do. The result is a much larger business volume achieved from even greater leverage and duplication, but with fewer people required to achieve it.

## #68   Using retail profit to help build your business

Most network marketing companies provide the opportunity for you to purchase the products they distribute at the wholesale price and sell at the retail price, thus creating retail profit for you on top of the remuneration available through their compensation and bonus scales. Of course, there will be some associated costs you will have to cover while building your business, such as educational and motivational material, business building tools and attending seminars, and incidental costs such as phone, fuel and other small home office operating costs. Generating retail profit from selling products is a great resource for covering these expenses. The retail profit available through selling product assists in funding the building of your business by covering some of the operating costs and thus minimising stress on your existing bank account.

This can take away the barrier faced by traditional business owners when they have to decide whether they can afford to buy this, or attend that. If you build your business in the correct way, you won't ever have to worry about whether to buy this, or attend that, because your business can pay for it through your retail profits.

# Notes on building a successful network marketing business

..............................................................
..............................................................
..............................................................
..............................................................
..............................................................
..............................................................
..............................................................
..............................................................
..............................................................
..............................................................
..............................................................
..............................................................
..............................................................
..............................................................
..............................................................
..............................................................
..............................................................
..............................................................
..............................................................
..............................................................

*One of the most important principles of success is developing the habit of going the extra mile.*
**Napoleon Hill**

# 9 | Prospecting, contacting and inviting

'Prospecting' is the term used in business to describe the process of identifying people potentially interested in whatever your business may be offering. In network marketing these will be people who may be interested in joining you in business or in buying product. Ongoing prospecting is an essential element of any business.

'Contacting and inviting' is the process of contacting those on your prospect list and inviting them to have a look at the opportunity. This is a crucial part of your business because the more people you can present the opportunity to, the better chance you have of finding the people who will be as excited as you are. This aspect can be very intimidating for those of us who struggle with the fear of contacting people and the fear of rejection.

This section focuses on developing and maintaining a list of prospects who may join you in business and become part of your team so that you can develop your network. It also looks at the contacting and inviting process; greater understanding of the process will help you to overcome some of the fears you may have.

#69 Making a list of prospects
#70 Never judge a book by its cover
#71 Continually add to your list
#72 Meet people, don't go out and hunt for people

## #69  Making a list of prospects

The first step in building your network marketing business is to make a list of all the people you know who you may be able to approach and ask to look at the idea. This is a very important step, but one that many people don't take the time to do; in not doing so, they get off to a bad start. If you want to build a successful network marketing business, you cannot underestimate the importance of this step. Understanding this, you will then promote its importance to your team as it grows. The power of this duplication will dramatically increase the speed at which your business builds.

To make your list, simply write down the names of everyone you have ever known or met. They may be family, friends, work colleagues, people you know on a casual basis. They don't have to be current contacts either; it doesn't matter if you haven't had contact with them for some time—if you've got a name, write it down. Most of the network marketing companies or their support systems will have a standard form to help you prepare your list, but if they don't you can very easily make up your own.

When you're making this list, don't be concerned about who might or might not be interested; that's a big mistake. At this stage you're simply putting together a list of everyone you have ever known. Just concentrate on making the list without relating it to the business. By not pre-judging people your mind will 'open the floodgates' so that every time you add a name it will help to remind you of another. If you are a couple building the business, put aside some time to work on your list together; do some brainstorming, pull out old mailing lists or invitation lists if you have them, old telephone directories, anything that might help to jog your memory.

The list you are making is setting the foundations of your business. The more names you have the stronger the foundation will be, and the larger the business that can be built upon it.

## #70  Never judge a book by its cover

It is amazing the number of people who, even after the importance of the list has been explained to them, end up with only a handful of names. The reason is that they are pre-judging people. Pre-judging is assuming that a particular person won't be interested in the business opportunity, for reasons such as: they might be too busy, they are doing okay anyway, or they wouldn't be interested in something like this. In some cases you might not add them because you're afraid of what they may think of you being involved in network marketing.

Pre-judging people is something you must be conscious of; it can lead to missing out on opportunities. A good case in point arises from Elise and Eddy, who were thinking about adding Miranda, who they hadn't been in contact with for some time, to their list. They pre-judged her—she's probably happy with what she's doing already, I don't think she would be interested, she's too busy. Six months later, at a local network marketing business seminar Elise and Eddy were attending, that same Miranda was being recognised on stage for her achievements. Introduced to network marketing by someone else, Miranda was already putting together a sizable team, even though she had been involved for only a short time.

Miranda and her husband went on to build a very successful and profitable business. When speaking to her after the seminar, it became very clear to Elise and Eddy that none of their pre-judgments of her were correct; the truth was quite the opposite.

Remember, your list at this stage is just that—a list. It does not mean you will be contacting all the people on it, but it gives you a strong foundation to work from. And consider how you would have felt if someone had pre-judged you and not given you the opportunity that you now have. The bottom line is that you have a great opportunity to share. At least give others the choice to make their own decision on becoming involved; don't make the decision for them.

## #71   Continually add to your list

An important point in building your business is to always be adding to your list. At times a name you initially overlooked will pop into your head; make sure you write it down somewhere straightaway, then add it to the list later. Don't rely on remembering it; nine times out of ten you will forget. Also, just because you have started your business doesn't mean you have stopped meeting people. As you meet new people, add them to your list; some of them may end up joining you in your business. The benefit of continually adding to your list is that you will never feel that your prospects are running out. The problem with starting with a small list and finding that most of the names are eliminated is that panic starts to set in—'How can I build the business without people to share it with?'

An important aspect of making and adding to your list is to understand that this step is the same when operating a traditional business. Traditional businesses rely on the number of leads they can generate, the number of people they can get to come through the door, the number of listings they can post, and so on. This is their 'names list', and they know that they have a certain conversion rate from names to sales. Your network marketing business is just the same, a business, and you too in time will have a certain conversion rate of names to sales. One thing is certain—just as in traditional business, if you don't have the names to begin with or you don't keep adding to your list, the chances of having a successful business will be substantially reduced.

## #72 Meet people, don't go out and hunt for people

A frequent misconception about adding to the names list is the belief that you must go out and 'get people'. Thinking this, you will get up in the morning with the goal of adding to your list, and go out to hunt for people. The end result is usually that you will return home without achieving your goal, and you will probably feel quite stressed out about the whole ordeal. In fact, adding to your list is not about hunting for people, but rather involves going about your normal routine while making a point of meeting new people. This means making a point of starting conversations and as a result getting to meet more people.

You don't have to view each new person you meet as a prospect with a bullseye painted on their forehead; just learn to converse more readily and make a friend. During your conversation take a genuine interest and ask questions. A formula often used is referred to by the acronym FORM: Family, Occupation, Recreation, Motivation. By asking questions around these subjects you may find people who are in the 'looking zone': people who might be interested in looking at what you are doing as a solution to a problem.

## #73   Inviting people to look at your business

Okay, you've developed your list of prospects. The next step is to contact them and invite them to have a look at what you are doing, with the view that it might be something that would interest them also. Many of the network marketing companies and their support systems have proven methods and techniques for contacting and inviting. The very best thing you can do is find out what those techniques are and simply duplicate them. As well, your coach or mentor can assist you in getting started. Be humble enough to become teachable, and listen to advice.

A good practice to live by when you're getting started is after contacting three prospects, stop and check your progress with your coach. If you are not getting the desired results, check your approach technique with your coach; there may be a very simple way of improving your results.

Allow yourself some time to get into the swing of things; don't expect to be an expert right from the word go as you could be setting yourself up for disappointment. All those things you've begun in your life—a new job, sport or hobby— you did not expect to be good at straightaway, and it's the same with your new business. Remember, practice makes perfect and consistency creates excellence.

## #74 Looking for lookers

Any business, including your network marketing business, is governed by the universal law that 'doing business is a numbers game'. The more you work the numbers the better your chances of winning the game. Any business, large or small, understands that not all the people who come through their doors, make enquiries, request quotes, or whom they cold contact to generate leads, will want what they have to offer. But they also understand that if they do enough, they will find the people who want what is offered. Your network marketing business is no different. If you understand right from the word go that not everyone is going to want what you have to offer, even though you may think they should, it will make your journey so much easier. The good news is, there are lots of people who will want it. Your job is simply to weed out the ones who will join you from the ones who won't.

At any given time, 10 per cent of the population is actively looking to make a change in their life, for whatever reason. It could be lack of money, job dissatisfaction, wanting their own business, concern about retirement—you name it. What you are trying to achieve when you contact people is to find those who are in the looking zone. Simply put, you are looking for lookers. Understanding this very important point will make building your network marketing business much more enjoyable and far less stressful. Many people struggle with the large number of rejections they get, seeing it as a reflection on the future success of the business. They have failed to grasp that in business, any business, you usually get more no's than yes's.

From the names list you've made, and from the people you add to it, you will find a percentage who are in the looking zone. You probably imagine you know who they're likely to be, but in lots of cases you will be surprised by who is and who isn't looking. It helps to develop the mindset that when contacting people you are looking for one of two responses, either a yes or

145

a no. Thinking like this means that every time you make a contact you will have a successful result. If you start making contact expecting that everyone will say yes, this is a false expectation, and one which can cause you much grief.

Your network marketing business is built on leverage and duplication. Its success, however, is largely based on your ability to get enough yes's, then teaching your yes's that same principle so that they can go out and get more yes's, and so on.

In quite a short time this can become a very large group of very excited people working towards achieving their dreams simply by getting lots of no's and just enough yes's. Remember, though, that getting enough yes's always involves getting a lot more no's. Let's look at the no's in a positive light—say you have built your business to a level that represents a passive income of $200 000 per year, and that along the way you had 1000 no's. Over ten years that income represents $2 000 000, which means that each of the no's you got was actually worth $2000. The more years at that income, or the larger the income, the greater the value of the no's. Obviously these numbers are rounded off to make the example easier to follow, but hopefully you can take from it the point that you can get excited about the no's as well as the yes's!

Don't see the no's as a non-result or a waste of time; see them as a very profitable investment of time while you're looking for lookers.

# #75  It's an invitation, not an explanation

One of the biggest mistakes that people make when inviting contacts to have a look at what they are doing is trying to explain the opportunity to them right there and then. It is important to remember this—the objective in making the initial contact with someone is simply to invite them to see what you are doing. Do not try to explain it at this time. Of course, people are naturally going to be curious when you contact them and will undoubtedly ask you questions—but hold back for now.

The reason for holding off answering their questions is that once you answer one question you will be asked others, so that before long you are trying to explain the whole idea. The result, more often than not, is that you will lose people because they cannot clearly see the opportunity in its entirety; they will make up their minds based on the small amount of information you've offered, rather than the whole picture.

The most useful technique to use in contacting people is often referred to as 'the curiosity approach'. Rather than trying to go into all the details, give just enough information during the contact to make the person curious to find out more. Many newcomers to network marketing struggle with this approach, perceiving it as somehow deceitful or dishonest. Understand that this is a normal business practice used extensively throughout the business world, both in network marketing and in traditional business. People in business understand that to do the right thing by your prospect you need to explain your product or service in detail face to face, in an environment which is both professional and businesslike. Your reason for contacting and inviting people is to do just that.

Also remember that you have a genuine opportunity to share with people. If you contact them incorrectly and they decide not to have a look, who has lost out? They have, because you never gave them the chance to sit down and see the opportunity in full so that they could make an informed decision. When you are contacting people, always remember that it's an invitation to your prospect to get together and find out more about what you have to offer, it's not an explanation of what you are doing.

# #76 Don't try to convince people

When inviting people to have a look at what you are doing, always remember that you are only looking for people who are themselves looking for something. If someone says they're not interested, then please, don't try to convince them otherwise. Most of the stigma associated with network marketing has been caused by people who just don't know how to take 'no' for an answer, who persistently badger their contacts in the hope they'll wear them down and change their minds. Remember, when you contact someone your goal is to find out whether they are open to having a look or not. If they're not, mission accomplished—it's been a successful contact because you have achieved your goal of a yes or no response.

As excited about the opportunity as you may be, understand that not everyone will see it the same way. This is quite natural, and does not reflect on you. And also, just because someone is a 'no' now doesn't necessarily mean they will be a 'no' forever. People can go in and out of several looking zones during their life. When someone says they are not interested, it is because they are happy with what they are doing at the moment and not looking for something else. With this in mind, when and if they do move into a looking zone, because you approached them the first time in a professional and businesslike manner they will be far more inclined to see you again because they respect the way you handle yourself.

# Notes on building a successful network marketing business

...................................................................

...................................................................

...................................................................

...................................................................

...................................................................

...................................................................

...................................................................

...................................................................

...................................................................

...................................................................

...................................................................

...................................................................

...................................................................

...................................................................

...................................................................

...................................................................

...................................................................

...................................................................

...................................................................

*Fear is never a reason for quitting;*
*it is only an excuse.*
**Norman Vincent Peale**

# 10 | Presenting your opportunity to others

You have contacted your prospect and organised a time to meet; now it's time to present your idea. Just like contacting a prospect, this can be daunting if you've never done it before. At the same time it can be very exciting. There is nothing more uplifting than seeing the spark ignite as your prospect starts to grasp the opportunity, to see that it may be a way for them too to achieve their dreams. This section covers the fundamentals of making a successful presentation.

# #77  It doesn't have to be perfect

Presenting your business to others simply means going through the opportunity with them and explaining the concept in detail. This can be done on a one-on-one basis or in a small group meeting in someone's home. The preferred method may vary from company to company, and in some cases may even involve public group meetings with a guest speaker doing the presentation. In the majority of cases you will be required to do a certain number of presentations yourself, again either on a one-on-one basis or in small group meetings, more than likely in the home of the prospect.

A stumbling block that many people face, particularly the perfectionist types, is believing they must get the presentation perfect before sharing it with their prospects. This can often result in a stalling of your business, because no one is being shown the opportunity while you are holding off, waiting to get it just right, or thinking you must know all the facts and figures before you start. Many network marketing companies or their support systems will have a proven presentation for you to follow, which may also be supported with presentation material. Always find out what is available to you, and take advantage of what is probably a tried and true method that works. Don't try to reinvent the wheel or give in to an 'I'll do it my way' impulse—follow the system if there is one.

Don't wait until you think you have all the answers or have a very rehearsed presentation, just make a start. The best way to learn is by doing—and remember, your prospect doesn't know what is right or wrong about your presentation, so it doesn't have to be perfect.

## #78   Be sure both partners are present

If you are presenting the opportunity to a couple, it's important that you make sure that both of them are present. You will often find that if you only show it to one of them and they get excited, they will then try to explain it to their partner when you are not there. In the majority of cases, they will not be able to explain it correctly or answer questions. The usual result is that you lose them, simply because the second partner has objected to something that the first could not clearly explain.

A good example of the importance of this is Louisa's story. She presented the opportunity to Julia without Julia's husband, Joe, being present. Julia got really excited about the idea and indicated to Louisa that she would get involved, although she wanted to talk to Joe about it first. Unfortunately, when she attempted her explanation, Joe asked her lots of questions and raised some concerns that she was unable to answer. When Louisa returned, Julia's response was, 'I have spoken to my husband about it and we have decided not to go ahead.' Louisa was obviously disappointed but, to rub salt into the wound, some months later she came across that same Julia and Joe at a local network marketing seminar. Joe had been shown the opportunity by a work colleague and decided they would get in straightaway. What's interesting is that when Julia told him that it was the same opportunity that she'd tried to explain to him earlier, Joe's response was, 'Well, it didn't sound anything like what I've seen.' The reality is, it probably didn't, because Julia wasn't Louisa and didn't have all the answers.

Something else to consider: because the network marketing opportunity you are offering can potentially have a very positive impact on those getting involved, both financially and personally, it is only fair when a couple is involved that both partners be present. When you make your contact and invitation to a couple, stress how important it is that they are both there, and organise the presentation to best suit both partners. Never allow yourself to be persuaded by the person you are contacting that it's okay just to see one of them; studies have shown that when this happens the percentage who decide to get involved is dramatically reduced.

## #79  Make a friend

If the people you are presenting to decide to join you in business, your association with them may be long and close. With this in mind, begin to develop a relationship before rushing into your presentation. Take some time to get to know them, show a genuine interest and ask questions. Look for things in their home that might indicate an interest in a sport or a hobby and ask questions about it. For example, lots of family photos on the wall probably indicate that they are very family orientated.

A word of warning: don't be false. People are very perceptive and today are very conscious of the typical 'sales' style. Always remember, 'people don't care how much you know until they know how much you care'. By taking the time to get to know your contacts a little better, you will find that they will be far more relaxed and less defensive once you get into your presentation. You will also find they will be far more open to talk about their dreams and goals, which is very important to the presentation.

Your network marketing business is a business of people. If you want to build a successful business, you need to have a genuine interest and build relationships with your people, which all starts at the first presentation.

## #80  Sell the dream, not the business

A very common mistake made in presentations is to spend the largest part of it on the logic of the business, on the facts and figures, on why it is such a great idea. Although important, these are not the reasons why most people get involved. The decision is usually an emotional one, responding to what they see they can get from the opportunity, not necessarily the opportunity itself. For many people, your presentation provides the chance of achieving dreams or goals which they feel can't be achieved by what they are currently doing. Ask yourself what the driving force was behind your own decision to get involved. Was it the logic of the business or the emotion of achieving your dream?

The majority of your presentation time should be taken up with trying to find out what your prospect would like to achieve outside of what they are currently doing. Your goal should be to find out what their dreams are, and then to talk about how the network marketing business opportunity can help them achieve those dreams. Presenting the opportunity is not about selling the business concept, but about showing your prospect how the business is a vehicle that can be used to achieve their dreams. It is more a dream-building session than a business explanation. If you finish your presentation not knowing what your prospect's dreams are, it is a good indication that you spent too much time on explaining and selling the business, not the dream.

Those who create the biggest organisations within network marketing do so by understanding the importance of the dream; they are often the biggest dream-builders. They have helped their people to identify their dreams, then constantly reminded them, and have helped them achieve them. Always remember, the business is simply a vehicle; the dream is what drives it; and like all vehicles, no matter how good it is, without fuel it's not going anywhere.

## #81   Don't suffer from detail-itis

During your presentation, don't fall into the trap of getting into too much detail, particularly information that the prospect does not need to know right now. At the first presentation your prospect just needs to know enough to satisfy their interest. Sometimes it is easy to get carried away and start telling them everything about every aspect of the business— before long your prospect will be overwhelmed by it all. What most prospects need to know is just enough to move them to the next stage, where they will have some questions, before getting started.

When presenting to a prospect who has a high level of interest and is getting excited, it's easy to make the mistake of getting carried away yourself instead of stopping right there. The presenter sees the enthusiasm shown by the prospect as a sign to tell them more, wrongly thinking that this will generate even more excitement. In fact it will be the opposite, the prospect losing interest because of information overload. In doing your presentation it's good practice to continually ask yourself, 'Does this person really need to know this just yet?' In the majority of cases the answer will be no. Developing this habit will greatly assist you, particularly in the early days, of not falling into the trap of overwhelming your prospects with irrelevant information.

## #82   Make the next appointment

When you have done your presentation and the prospect has shown a degree of interest, organise your next meeting with them. Always have your diary with you so you can organise it there and then. Try to get back to them within the next 48 hours if possible. You will find that people's enthusiasm and interest will start to wane after that time. If you have follow-up material, leave it with them; this will assist in maintaining their interest level.

This is a very important step in the process; it is easy in all the excitement to walk out the door without making the next appointment. What can sometimes happen is that you can feel as though you are 'chasing' the prospect when you ring up to get together again. Try to remember to 'book a meeting from a meeting', which simply means that before leaving the current meeting you book the next one. Your prospects will also respect this professional and organised approach.

## #83  Overcoming objections

In presenting any idea in any context you will always be confronted with the occasional objection. In business, any business, it is even more common. Network marketing is no different and you will find as you build your business that a series of common objections will come up quite frequently. The objections may vary depending on the type of network marketing company you are affiliated with, but over time you will see a regular pattern of objections specific to what you are proposing.

The good news is that they are normally restricted to half a dozen or so. More good news is that objections are not necessarily a negative, in fact they can be quite positive. As you build your business it is important that you don't let objections affect your attitude. Instead, learn to identify the objections, what they really mean, and how to turn them into opportunities.

A page is provided at the end of this section where you can note down the most common objections you come across when presenting your idea to others. Note down beneath each one the response that you have found works best for you or has been recommended by your coach. You can then use this page as a reference to come back to and review the best responses to the most common objections.

## #84 Objections are sometimes questions in disguise

Some of the objections you will come across may include: I don't think I have the time; I don't think I could do what you do; I don't think I would know anybody interested; and so on. Sometimes objections are actually questions in disguise, and what your prospect is in fact saying is, 'I'm interested, but I don't think I have the time—can you tell me that is not a problem?' Your job is to find out whether the objection is a genuine objection and your prospect is saying no to the idea as a result, or whether it is a question in disguise and your prospect is saying yes if you have a positive answer.

The only way to determine this is to ask. A good way of doing this is to say, 'If I can help you overcome that, would you then be interested in getting started?' Their response will assist you in knowing what to do next. Without asking, you will never know whether it is a genuine objection or a question in disguise, which hinders your ability to make the presentation a success.

## #85   Is it an objection or an excuse?

Some people can find it difficult to just say no when they are
not interested in the opportunity. To avoid saying no, they will
use an objection as an excuse. The end result of the 'objection'
is the same as that of a genuine objection: they are a no.

Nevertheless, it's important to be aware of the difference
between the two so that you better understand the reasons
behind people's decisions. To determine the real reason behind
the objection, once again ask the question: 'If I can help you
overcome that, would you then be interested in getting
started?' Their response will help you determine what to do
next; if their response is no, the objection is either genuine or
an excuse. Either way, they will not be getting started with you.

## #86 Learning to overcome objections

Overcoming objections is a skill which can be learnt. For some people it comes easily, for others it can take a little time. In either case the best move you can make is to have a coach or mentor in your up-line who you can look to for advice. Your coach or mentor is your best resource in learning to overcome objections because they have 'been there and done that' and have 'heard them all before'. Don't make the mistake of being confronted with the same objections time after time—affecting your success rate—without asking your coach or mentor to assist you.

It is vital that you put aside any pride or ego when it comes to learning to overcome objections. Become a student and actively look for assistance wherever you can. Fortunately, the objections that most people put forward are fairly predictable and number just a few, so it is a case of learning how to overcome them. Over time you will develop an arsenal of responses to the common and not-so-common objections.

## #87  Leading people from objections to getting started

Quite often people who are interested in what you are offering will tell you so through their body language or their questions, rather than openly saying, 'Let's get started'. Because they are really saying 'yes', but waiting for you to lead them, it is important that you recognise these 'buying signals'. It's not difficult, in most cases you will intuitively respond to the feeling that these people are interested. When this happens, lead them into getting started by moving on to the next stage in the process, like doing paperwork, starting their names list or organising a meeting with their friends. Remember, your prospects do not know what the next step is; they are relying on you to lead them. Holding off at this point because you think it's too pushy to suggest something to the prospect is a mistake. In fact, the prospect is waiting, even hoping, for the suggestion.

A story to highlight this is that of Brian. He'd shown the opportunity to Gail, who'd responded with a high level of interest. At the end of the meeting Brian left Gail some information and organised to follow up in a couple of days. At that meeting Gail still appeared highly interested and had more questions. Again Brian left her with information, and organised to meet again in a couple of days. This happened twice more. When Brian was meeting with his up-line coach, he mentioned his progress, or lack thereof, with Gail. Puzzled by this story, Brian's coach suggested he come along to the next scheduled meeting. Gail's remaining questions were quickly covered and the coach, sensing her interest, simply led her into getting started and doing the paperwork.

The most important element of this story is what happened next: after completing the paperwork Gail put down her pen and said, 'Thank heavens, I've been wanting to do that for two weeks.' As it turned out she'd been ready to get started back at the first follow-up visit. When Brian suggested leaving her more information she'd assumed that must be the next step, and so on.

Understand that you are leading people, not pushing them; people cannot be led if they don't want to be, and if you have misinterpreted the buying signal they will tell you. There are countless stories in network marketing of people like Gail who want to get started but are frustrated by people like Brian who think they want more time to consider it or need more information.

People will often rely on you to lead them to get started based on their buying signals, rather than saying so openly. If you have presented the opportunity to someone and you feel they are interested, don't be frightened to lead them into getting started by suggesting what they should do next.

**Common objections**

1) Objection: ..............................................................

   Response: ..............................................................

   ..............................................................

   ..............................................................

   ..............................................................

2) Objection: ..............................................................

   Response: ..............................................................

   ..............................................................

   ..............................................................

   ..............................................................

3) Objection: ..............................................................

   Response: ..............................................................

   ..............................................................

   ..............................................................

   ..............................................................

4) Objection: ..............................................................

   Response: ..............................................................

   ..............................................................

   ..............................................................

   ..............................................................

# Notes on building a successful network marketing business

..................................................................

..................................................................

..................................................................

..................................................................

..................................................................

..................................................................

..................................................................

..................................................................

..................................................................

..................................................................

..................................................................

..................................................................

..................................................................

..................................................................

..................................................................

..................................................................

..................................................................

..................................................................

..................................................................

..................................................................

..................................................................

*Success does not consist in never making mistakes but in never making the same one a second time.*
**George Bernard Shaw**

# 11 | Some of the challenges we all face in network marketing

Network marketing is a great opportunity but it does not come without some challenges. The first step when dealing with challenges is to understand that they are normal. In this section we look at some of the most common challenges that you will encounter in network marketing, particularly those which tend to affect people's attitude the most. Learning to recognise these challenges and how to respond to them will make your journey in building your business so much more rewarding.

#88 Coping with rejection
#89 The people factor
#90 Disappointment is part of the game
#91 Politics
#92 People's perceptions
#93 Negativity from those closest to you
#94 You won't always hit your goals

## #88   Coping with rejection

It's our natural disposition to want people to like us and to agree with us, and we want to fit in. When people reject us, or an idea we are proposing, we tend to take it personally.

Unfortunately, to succeed in business, any business, you will also need to face rejection repeatedly. Because of this you will have to recognise that rejection is a normal part of doing business, and then learn how to handle it. Being in business means you are in the business of numbers and doing business is a numbers game: the more you work the numbers the better chance you have of winning the game. Your network marketing business is no different, and to work the numbers you will naturally be exposed to large numbers of rejections.

There are possibly a few exceptions, but in general successful people will tell you that they've never really got to feel comfortable with rejection but rather have learnt to understand it as a normal part of business and to not take it personally; they understand that it is part of the success formula.

Many who have failed in network marketing have done so because they had difficulty in coming to terms with this reality. In an effort to avoid the rejection they failed to undertake the activities required to build their business. If you are going to make a success of your business the good news is that you don't have to totally conquer the feelings associated with rejection, but rather learn how to cope with them. Recognise that rejection is a normal part of doing business and part of the price you pay for success.

## #89  The people factor

Developing a network marketing business involves developing a network of people who will represent a vast array of backgrounds, ages, nationalities and personalities. Few of them will be like you, or have the same likes and dislikes as you do. This means you must be able to deal with and relate to a large cross-section of society and have the ability to accept people for who they are.

In developing a successful network marketing business you place yourself in a position of leadership that will sometimes require you to organise your team collectively. The cross-section of society and the variety of personalities in your team in itself can cause some frustration. As your network and the diversity of people within it grow, the demands on you to cater to their attitudes and problem-solving abilities also increases. Many will bring with them baggage from the past such as relationship issues, past failures and lack of confidence, alongside the day-to-day challenges we all face.

You must understand that you cannot please everyone and nor can you solve all their problems. The best you can do is try to meet people where they are at and be a friend. The best response to the challenge of dealing with people is to improve your people skills. There are many excellent books on the topic that are well worth the investment. One of the best ever written is Dale Carnegie's *How to Win Friends and Influence People*. While some may think the title sounds manipulative, this book simply teaches you to be a better communicator, to create deeper connections with others, to avoid—and, if necessary, resolve—conflict, and generally have more open and honest interactions.

Often spending the time to review your own personal communication skills, traits and general attitude is the best place to start improving your communication with others. We have found that being genuinely interested in the lives of others is of major benefit in this process.

# #90 Disappointment is part of the game

In developing any network of people for whatever reason, there will always be times when some of those people will disappoint you. Not all the people who join you in your network marketing business will stay with you. Some, even those who you have spent a lot of time and effort assisting and encouraging, will decide not to remain involved. Others who back out may even include those who you thought were going to be key people, an integral part of your own business structure in achieving your goals. Others will simply not be as active as you would like them to be. Some will say one thing and do another.

There will be those who will disappoint you by not being as loyal as you would expect after you have spent time, money and energy in assisting them to build their business. Some may even defect to another leader higher in your organisation, perhaps to satisfy their own egos.

The good news is that these people make up only a small percentage of what is a very large network and you must recognise that it is an unavoidable element in your business. The trick is to understand that it's not about what happens to you, but how you react to it.

## #91  Politics

Whenever you have a large group of people within an organisation, as that organisation grows the element of politics will inevitably grow also. Politics within large groups usually revolves around people forming into smaller groups. Over time this can manifest itself as the 'us and them' syndrome. Politics is not unique to network marketing and you need to understand that it forms part of any large business organisation. Favouritism, stepping on toes, gossip, petty competition and miscommunication are just a few examples of what takes place as politics increases.

Politics can arise within your own team, between your team and another, between the leaders in the business, between the company itself and its support systems, or between company representatives and business owners.

It is important to understand that this aspect of your business is not a negative, but just one of the challenges of building any successful business, whether it be a traditional business or a network marketing business.

## #92   People's perceptions

People have many perceptions of network marketing, some positive, others negative. The nay-sayers are almost invariably ill-informed and unqualified to say the things they do, but they say them just the same. You are going to have to deal with their negativity if you are to make a success of your network marketing business. Worrying about how people perceive your business and what they think of you being involved will certainly lead to failure. But if you talk to successful people in sport or business, you will find that all have been faced with negative perceptions from others.

One of the biggest causes of failure in network marketing is not that the business did not work, but that those involved never got to work the business because of worrying about what others thought of them.

## #93   Negativity from those closest to you

Sadly, some of your biggest critics can be family and friends. Sibling rivalry and jealousy can play a part in how people react to your involvement in network marketing. Quite often people don't want you to succeed because it would show them up as not willing to chase their own dreams. Other cases reflect genuine concern on the part of those close to you, because they don't want you to be hurt or disappointed if it doesn't work out. They might have preconceived ideas about network marketing and be carrying those over to your involvement.

Whatever the reasons, be prepared for possible negative reactions from friends and family. It can be difficult at times, but you must understand that their thoughts and suggestions should not be taken personally. More importantly, they should not be a reason for you not to pursue the opportunity. Don't try to convince them, or get into an argument over the difference of opinion. Just understand that they simply don't know what you know, and realise this is just one of the prices to pay for success. The very best thing you can do to prove you are right is to achieve success—go on and build your network marketing business and in time you'll find they've become your biggest supporters.

Everyone who has achieved any level of success in their endeavours, particularly those with a business idea, has undoubtedly been faced with a degree of doubt and negativity among family and friends. One of the biggest reasons a lot of people never reach the level of success they are capable of achieving is that they never get beyond conforming to the opinions and restraints put upon them by others. The question you need to ask yourself is: 'Are the opinions of others important enough to stop me from possibly achieving my dreams?'

## #94   You won't always hit your goals

One of the hardest things for people to come to grips with as they build their network marketing business is not achieving all the goals they've set for themselves. Many see it as failure, and the more goals they don't hit, the more of a failure they feel. To be successful, whether it is in business, sport or your personal life, the reality is that you will miss your goals more often than hitting them. Understanding this principle will make the journey of building your business so much easier. Goals are simply the path to your true destination: your dream. Missing some of your goals does not mean you cannot reach your destination, it just means resetting the path to get there.

It will always be disappointing when you don't achieve a particular goal, but if you know in your heart that you did all you could to make it happen, that's good enough. Not achieving your goals is not the problem—the problem comes when you don't pick yourself up, dust yourself down, reset your goals and move on. Almost all who have achieved some level of success will tell you 'they failed their way to success'. They understood the importance of resetting their goals and never giving up. You too will miss a lot of your goals as you build your network marketing business, but like all those before you who have failed their way to success and achieved their dreams, you will succeed if you never lose sight of your dreams and never give up.

# Notes on building a successful network marketing business

..........................................................................

..........................................................................

..........................................................................

..........................................................................

..........................................................................

..........................................................................

..........................................................................

..........................................................................

..........................................................................

..........................................................................

..........................................................................

..........................................................................

..........................................................................

..........................................................................

..........................................................................

..........................................................................

..........................................................................

..........................................................................

..........................................................................

*The greatest discovery of my generation is that a human being can alter his life by altering his attitudes of mind.*
**William James**

# 12 | Attitude—it's only everything

Talk to any successful person and they will tell you that a key ingredient of success is attitude. Your attitude can literally determine your destiny. It is the one thing that you have total control over, that no one can take from you—unless you let them. A major factor in succeeding in network marketing is a positive attitude throughout the journey: no one has ever gone on to build a successful network marketing business with a bad attitude. We all have the potential for greatness within us; attitude is the foundation on which that potential can be built. In this section we discuss the importance of attitude, how to control it and how to protect it.

#95 If you think you can, you can—if you think you can't, you can't
#96 Don't sweat the small stuff
#97 Surround yourself with positive people
#98 Read positive, reinforcing books
#99 Stay away from negative influences
#100 The power of being consistent
#101 Never give up

## #95  If you think you can, you can—if you think you can't, you can't

If there is one single defining ingredient in the formula for success it would have to be attitude. Your attitude can literally determine your destiny, thus it is critical that you understand the importance of its effect on you and on your performance. The great news is that you—and only you—can choose what you want your attitude to be: negative or positive. It may take some practice to be able to make the mindshift when you feel yourself slipping into negative, but it can be done.

Having a positive attitude is simply seeing the good and the possibilities in every situation. There are countless clichés when it comes to having a positive attitude, such as whether you see the glass as half-full or half-empty. Most of them have an element of truth. All successful people, in whatever field, will tell you that the biggest single element that has led them to their success has been their attitude—'it's only everything'.

Developing a good attitude takes work, in some cases a lot of work, but first you must make the decision to work on it. If you want to build a really successful network marketing business and at the same time have a rounded personal life, the best place to start is perfecting a positive attitude. The exciting news is, you can learn how to control your attitude. It is the one thing that no one else can have control over. You can decide how to be affected by someone or something. You have total control. If you need help, there are countless books on attitude available. More than likely you will be able to get some of these through your network marketing business or its support system. To get you started, we particularly recommend *Attitude is Everything* by Jeff Keller and *Success Through a Positive Mental Attitude* by Napoleon Hill.

## #96   Don't sweat the small stuff

*Rule #1: Don't sweat the small stuff;*
*Rule #2: It's all small stuff.*

As your network marketing business is just that, a business, it is important to understand that not everything will go smoothly all of the time. There will always be times when things will not go according to plan. There may be delivery delays, incorrect dispatching, out of stock items and so on. As a business owner it is critical you don't fall victim to small thinking and start sweating the small stuff, that you keep looking at the big picture and not at the problem. Many people who come into network marketing do so with very little or no business background and thus don't recognise that, inevitably, things can and do go wrong when running a business. Sometimes they lose it altogether and have an 'attitude attack' because of a minor problem, such as a dint or scratch on a product, or a product that has gone out of stock, or some other minor thing, which when compared with the bigger picture is insignificant.

As a business owner it is important that you learn to be proactive in resolving problems, not reactive. Become a problem solver rather than dwelling on the problem and getting bogged down in it.

## #97  Surround yourself with positive people

Most parents concern themselves with who their children associate with, fearing the effect on them of mixing with the 'wrong crowd'. Yet for some reason, as adults we tend to forget that same principle. Just like children, if we mix with negative, unenthusiastic and unambitious people, there is a very good chance we too will be influenced.

Successful people everywhere understand that to protect your attitude you must spend time with like-minded people who have a positive outlook on life. The more you can associate with positive people the more positive the effect it will have on you. A great benefit of network marketing is the positive environment it creates. Many of those involved are upbeat and optimistic, and the industry itself is strong on promoting positivity.

Be conscious of those around you who can have a negative effect on your attitude; spend the greatest part of your time with positive, uplifting people. The leaders within your network marketing business will be leaders because of their positive attitude; seek them out.

## #98  Read positive, reinforcing books

It is often said that 'leaders are readers', and that the books they read are positive, uplifting, personal development books. Many successful people are readers, in many cases prolific readers. Bookstores are full of helpful books, and many of the network marketing companies or their support systems will be good sources as well. If you're not a reader yourself, it really is important that you make a start. You don't have to go out and buy a whole bunch of books straightaway and read them overnight. A good starting point is to make a commitment to read at least fifteen minutes each day from a positive, reinforcing book. You will be amazed at the effect it will have on your attitude and your overall outlook on life.

In time you will find your fifteen minutes a day will increase, as you develop a hunger for more. You will see a noticeable improvement in your attitude and the flow-on effect on your business will be measurable. If you're not sure which books to read, ask your coach or mentor to recommend some. They will probably know which books you are likely to relate to, so that you will get the most out of your reading time.

## #99   Stay away from negative influences

If by some mischance you have family, friends or associates who are negative by nature, try to distance yourself from their negativity as much as possible. Negative often begets negative, and you need to protect your positive attitude as much as possible. This doesn't mean you never see them again, but it does mean being mindful of the influence their negativity can have on you and so limiting your exposure to it.

Also try to avoid negativity in the media—TV news programs, magazines or newspapers. We know that 'bad news sells', and quite often the media is full of negative news. This doesn't mean never watching TV or reading a newspaper, but do it in moderation due to the depressing effect bad news can have on your attitude. Don't worry, if there is something so bad that you need to know about it, someone will tell you!

# #100 The power of being consistent

A very common mistake while building a network marketing business is to work at it inconsistently. Making spasmodic focused efforts at building a business, but failing to maintain those efforts for any length of time, results in a business which never seems to develop any momentum. What also tends to happen is that a lot of what is being learnt in the doing is lost once the doing stops. What these people fail to recognise is that every time they start again, that's exactly what they're doing—they're starting again from the beginning, not from where they last stopped. Some of them may have been in their business for a long time, but in real time they have only been building their business for just a short period.

As your network marketing business is just that, a business, what is required here is some perspective. For example, if you were to start a traditional business but worked it inconsistently, how successful would you expect that business to be? If you ran a retail store that was open some days and closed others, how successful could you expect it to be?

If you are going to work your business then work it on a consistent basis. Decide how much time you are prepared to give it per week, then maintain that level of activity on an ongoing basis. If it's one day a week, then maintain that one day a week; obviously the more time the better but whatever it is, do it consistently. Businesses are built on momentum; you cannot create momentum if you are inconsistent.

Consistency gets you in a zone, lessons learnt are applied and not lost, ongoing activity leads to results, results lead to growth, growth transfers to excitement, excitement is contagious, which leads to others in your organisation duplicating you—and others duplicating you leads to even greater growth and excitement. All of which leads to building a very large network marketing business quickly; but it all started with you being consistent.

## #101  Never give up

During the course of building your business you will be confronted with challenges and disappointment. Your choice at these points of frustration will be whether to charge ahead regardless of the challenges, to grind to a halt or, worse, to give up altogether. To be successful in any endeavour requires you to be persistent and maintain a 'never give up' attitude. Be assured, the majority of successful people whom you respect and aspire to be like have all had their own challenges and disappointments along the way, possibly more than the average person would endure. What got them there in the end was their positive attitude, combined with persistence. It doesn't mean that they never thought of quitting—they would all admit that there were times when it crossed their minds—but it was the decision not to fall victim to a quitter's mentality that brought success.

You too will more than likely be faced with the same decision from time to time; it is at this point that the difference between winners and losers is defined. The winners of the world are the ones who persisted despite the setbacks. Understand also that success is often more about persistence than ability. What you may lack in natural ability can be learnt through persistence. Many sporting greats can tell stories of people they trained with or competed against in the early days of their careers whose natural ability was far superior to their own, but who lacked persistence.

As you build your business, make the decision that you will persist no matter what. Decide that you will build it with a better attitude than anybody else, and that you will continually work on improving your attitude. Decide right from the start that you will never give up.

# Notes on building a successful network marketing business

..........................................................................
..........................................................................
..........................................................................
..........................................................................
..........................................................................
..........................................................................
..........................................................................
..........................................................................
..........................................................................
..........................................................................
..........................................................................
..........................................................................
..........................................................................
..........................................................................
..........................................................................
..........................................................................
..........................................................................
..........................................................................
..........................................................................
..........................................................................

*Your attitude, not your aptitude, will determine your altitude.*

**Zig Ziglar**

# Twenty bonus tips for building your network marketing business

The bonus section has become a popular feature of the *101 Ways* series. It is designed not only to add value, but also provides a place for some extra ideas spanning all the categories covered earlier. The ideas we'll cover in this section are:

#102 Never stop learning

#103 Be a person of your word

#104 Opinions versus facts

#105 Don't become a networking fanatic

#106 Criticism means you're on track

#107 What other people think about you is none of your business

#108 Status will keep you broke

#109 Be organised

#110 Don't let your past hold you back

#111 Never, ever, pass negativity on to your team

#112 Become a good student so you can become a great teacher

#113 Don't become one of those 'in everything but not committed to anything' people

#114 Practise delayed gratification

#115 Make money, make a friend and make a difference

#116 Be loyal to your organisation

#117 Stay up to date on who's who in your business

#118 Structure your business to be profitable

#119  Give and you will receive
#120  Quitters never win and winners never quit
#121  In the end, 'if it has to be, it's up to me'

# #102  Never stop learning

In your business, as in life, you should never stop learning. There is much danger in thinking you know everything you need to know. As your business grows and the number of people involved increases, so also will the need to broaden your people skills, your leadership skills, your knowledge of business management and finances, increase. The network marketing industry is a unique 'university' of learning and you should embrace the opportunity to continually take advantage of it.

As your business grows, new products and services may become available, new and exciting tools, better ways of doing things. It is vital that you stay abreast of any changes and developments that can affect your business. The danger in not doing so is a business that becomes stale and stagnant. Always be willing to learn new things; don't let yourself become too comfortable with the knowledge you already have and feel that it will get you by. In the majority of businesses you are either going forwards or backwards; it is very difficult to maintain the status quo. Always keep learning how to develop personally as well. Again, the network marketing industry is a great environment for personal development.

It is often said that your income can be in direct relation to the books you read and the people you associate with. For some this can be a scary thought, and may be the reason they are not better off financially. Reading positive and motivating books and associating with positive, motivated and successful people both provide you with the opportunity to learn and grow beyond where you are now and in turn grow your income.

## #103  Be a person of your word

Building a network of people into a successful network marketing business results in quite a large organisation, and you will be required to take on a certain level of leadership as that organisation grows. Some people will revel in the leadership role and continue to play a very prominent part throughout the life of their business, while others may find it somewhat intimidating, playing their part in the short term but happy to take a back seat and hand over the long-term role to someone else.

Whatever the level of leadership you choose to take on, it is important that you understand that this role brings with it responsibility. One of the responsibilities is a simple one, but no less important for that, and that is to be a person of your word. If you tell someone that you are going to do something, do it. If you say you will be somewhere at a certain time, be on time.

More importantly, if you are telling your team you are striving for a certain goal or new level within your business, then go for it. It doesn't matter if you don't reach it as long as those you told see that you kept your word and gave it your best shot. Keeping your word builds trust, confidence, dependability and reliability in your team. People will know that they can count on you, which is a key ingredient in developing any successful team.

## #104  Opinions versus facts

As you start to build your network marketing business you are going to be confronted with all kinds of opinions about what you do. In the early days this can be dangerous because, being new to the industry and not yet knowing all the facts, you are more susceptible to being affected by mistaken opinions. Being vulnerable to the opinions of others in the early days of their business, many newcomers have unfortunately decided not to continue.

If at any time you are questioning your involvement because of an opinion that someone has put to you, before you do anything else, do some homework and get the facts. Go to the leaders in your organisation and put to them what has been said to you and listen to their response. Most often it will be an opinion they have heard a hundred times before and they will be able to quickly counteract it with the facts.

Interestingly, many who put forward negative opinions are not qualified to do so, either knowing very little about network marketing or never having been involved. Quite often their opinions are second-hand, even third-hand. When you are confronted in this way, the first thing to do is to ask yourself, 'How qualified is this person to give such an opinion? And why should an unqualified opinion have any bearing on my future success?'

## #105 Don't become a networking fanatic

You have every reason to be excited and enthusiastic about your network marketing business but be careful you don't turn into a fanatic. Some of the stigma associated with network marketing is in reaction to people who've become fanatical about their business and alienated those around them because 'all they ever do is rave on about their business, they never shut up about it'.

Remember that it's very important to keep a balance in your life between your network marketing business and your family, friends and other interests. Don't turn into someone who everyone runs and hides from whenever they see you coming because they know exactly what you are going to talk about. Treat your network marketing business as you would a traditional business. Approach it and those around you in a professional manner. This does not mean that you never talk about your business, but just be aware of over-stepping the boundaries.

## #106 Criticism means you're on track

It was once reported that Walt Disney often gathered his team around him and outlined a new idea he had. Interestingly, if the majority thought it was not a good idea, or even thought it was crazy, he would go ahead with it. Walt Disney's logic was simple; if everyone disagrees with and criticises what you are doing, you must be on the right track because you are doing something that others are not prepared to do. In other words, if you're doing something that everybody else is doing, you'll end up where everyone else is heading. If you do the opposite, you'll end up where most can only hope to be.

The majority of people live an average life, what is often referred to as being 'uncomfortably comfortable'. They would 'like' to make some changes but they're not prepared to go outside their comfort zone.

Your decision to become involved in network marketing puts you into the small percentage of people who are prepared to step outside their comfort zone and take a risk. In essence, you are doing what most people are not prepared to do and you should be congratulated for it.

## #107 What other people think about you is none of your business

One of the biggest factors holding people back from going on to build a successful network marketing business is a constant concern about what others think of them being involved. The fear of what other people think is one of the most common constraints people put on themselves. And it is not unique to network marketing.

Understand this: 'what other people think about you is none of your business'. What is important is what *you* think. What other people think about you should not control your destiny. If it did, half the successful people in the world would not be where they are today. Worrying about what people think is a sure-fire way of failing to achieve your dreams and goals—and not just in your network marketing business, but in life.

## #108  Status will keep you broke

A great danger in today's society is the 'keeping up with Joneses' mentality that people fall into, continually trying to outdo one another to develop some type of superior 'status'. The danger here, where network marketing is concerned, is that some people worry that their status will be threatened if others know they are involved. This is a hangover from the bad old days, when network marketing was unregulated, and seen as something you did as a last resort, only if you were desperate. It is very important that you understand this is not the case today. Network marketing is evolving into a mainstream business alternative, with many Fortune 500 companies looking to utilise network marketers as their distribution source.

If you are feeling uncomfortable about your involvement because of what others will think and the effect it may have on your standing, then you are suffering from a chronic bout of status-itis. The bottom line is that status-itis will keep you broke. Trying to maintain perceived status is often a big factor holding people back from achieving their potential.

## #109 Be organised

Being in business, any business, requires you to be organised. You will only get so far with sloppy business practice—in the end it will catch up with you big-time. Depending on your personality, being organised can come easily or be a real struggle. If you are a naturally organised type you won't need to spend much time grasping the importance of this tip. But if you are not so well organised, now is the time to address the problem. This doesn't mean you are required to go from one extreme to another overnight, but it does mean recognising that you need to focus on being better organised in the future.

If it were only you in business for yourself, and the only person you had to work with is yourself, you might get away with being disorganised—but you are building a network marketing business. If your goal is to build a successful business, you will be developing a large team. To deal with a large team requires you to be better organised, whether you like it or not. The easiest thing to do is to be organised right from the word go. If you wait till you are further down the track you will need to work hard to clean up the mess.

## #110  Don't let your past hold you back

Those who come into the network marketing industry do so from a wide range of ages, nationalities, educational levels, occupations and backgrounds. They will also have had varying levels of success in their former occupations. Some are fortunate enough to have some success already under their belt, but there will be others who have not been so fortunate, and in fact may be carrying a certain amount of baggage from previous failures.

There will also be those whose environment to date has not been a fertile one in terms of being exposed to success, encouragement, recognition or even education. A great feature of network marketing is that it is very much a level playing field which allows all who enter it an opportunity to succeed no matter what their past. Certainly, those who are not shackled by their past will probably reach their goals earlier, but the opportunity also means that everyone can succeed.

As you start to build your business, see it as a new beginning; don't see your past as a reason why you can't go on and build a successful business.

## #111 Never, ever, pass negativity on to your team

One of the attractive features of network marketing for many people is the positive environment, which they find uplifting, a pleasant change to the often negative environment found in their workplaces, and in some cases in their home lives. With this in mind, do not dilute this positive environment by passing on negativity to your team. If you have problems personally, financially or in your business, the best people to talk to are the people above you in your organisation, the leaders, not those below you in your team. If you have something you need to get off your chest, pass it up-line, not down-line.

Negativity is a very powerful state of mind. It is contagious, it demotivates, it makes people feel bad about all aspects of their life—and it is bad for your health. Learning to keep negativity at bay is a great life skill which will certainly help you to build a great business.

## #112 Become a good student so you can become a great teacher

Building a successful network marketing business is really about building a network of people and helping them become successful. Many of these people will look to you for leadership and advice, thus it is important that you have a good understanding of what it takes to build a successful business so you can teach others in your team to do the same. When starting your business, the quicker you can humble yourself and become a good student, the quicker you will gain the knowledge that will allow you to become a great teacher.

As network marketing is very much about others duplicating what you do, if you embrace a student mentality as quickly as possible your team will follow your lead and do the same, so that they too will better understand what is required to make a success of their business. Knowledge leads to confidence, confidence leads to action and action leads to results. The quicker you can gain the knowledge, the quicker you can pass on that knowledge, which leads to your whole team having confidence—which will create a team with lots of results.

## #113 Don't become one of those 'in everything but not committed to anything' people

If you know that you can be distracted or seduced to some extent by every new idea you are presented with, be careful you don't become one of those 'in everything but not committed to anything' people. People who swap and change and come in and out of every new idea they see rarely make a success of anything because they never stick at something long enough to make it work.

As for any business, making a success of your network marketing business requires you to make a commitment to stick it out and see it through. The world is full of people who were once involved in network marketing and never made any money. Many of them were looking for a quick fix and easy money. Once they'd found out that it takes work and commitment to make a success of it, they left in the hope of finding quick riches somewhere else.

# #114 Practise delayed gratification

Delayed gratification is simply delaying buying something until you can afford it, or delaying rewarding yourself for a goal you've set until you actually achieve it. Unfortunately, very few people practise delayed gratification. Today's society is very much 'buy now, pay later', encouraging people to reward themselves now and worry about paying for it later. This is a dangerous mindset and is not sustainable.

The single biggest reason for taking up the 'buy now, pay later' option is because a lack of disposable income does not encourage people to save and buy later. This, combined with our 'have it now' culture, has placed people into an enormous debt spiral. The good news is that your involvement in network marketing can break this cycle, putting you in a position where you can increase your disposable income and so save for things, buying them when you have the money together rather than going into debt.

In terms of waiting to reward themselves for achieving a goal they had set, many people reward themselves whether they reach the goal or not. Practising delayed gratification is a discipline, and a difficult one at times, but the rewards are enormous. If you have something you want to purchase, why not put off buying for now, and set yourself a goal related to your network marketing business. The end result will be having the ability to pay cash, combined with an enormous sense of achievement because the purchase has been combined with the reward for achieving the goal.

## #115 Make money, make a friend and make a difference

A very rewarding aspect of being involved in network marketing is the friendships that you can develop combined with the sense of achievement you feel in playing a part in helping others achieve their dreams and goals. In many respects, your success is about you making money by making friends and making a difference in their lives. A successful network marketing business is fundamentally built by you taking your eyes off yourself and focusing on others in your team. By helping others get what they want, you have the opportunity to get whatever you want.

## #116 Be loyal to your organisation

In most cases, involvement in network marketing means that you will be part of an organisation that is just one among many within the company you are affiliated with. Be aware of the risk of comparing your particular organisation with another in the company, particularly the leadership of your company. Be proud of the organisation or line of sponsorship you are part of; don't fall into the trap of the 'grass always being greener' elsewhere. More importantly, be loyal. Not being loyal to your organisation sends the wrong message to your team and can quickly erode all the good work you have done in developing it.

Always promote the leadership of your organisation to your team and emphasise how lucky you are to have those people up-line. Build confidence in your team by always praising your organisation, and not comparing it to others. In doing this you will empower your team with confidence and pride. Everyone likes to be part of a winning team; being loyal to your organisation helps to build this, for in the end, as we keep saying, it's teamwork that makes the dream work.

## #117 Stay up to date on who's who in your business

Your network will be made up of people with various levels of enthusiasm, activity, teachability, leadership and urgency. Some will be very active, others not so active. In other words, there will be people who want to build their business fast and those who don't. Those who want to build fast are your key people, and for your business to move quickly it is important that you know who they are. The time you allocate to helping and coaching others needs to be directed more to those who are looking for assistance.

One of the common mistakes in building a network marketing business lies in not knowing who your key people are. This can result in you spending enormous amounts of time trying to motivate everyone to do something which many of them don't yet wish to do. Identifying your key people will help you better manage your time and allow you to provide quality advice to those who want it.

To understand who your key people are, you must continually update yourself on who is in your business. You can try drawing up a 'family tree' of your team on a regular basis, but you will find this difficult once the organisation gets larger. Some network marketing companies have ways of tracking a team, perhaps in the form of a regular report they supply you with, or accessible through a web-based environment.

A great software tool developed specifically for the network marketing industry is a program developed by the Australian-based company WorXSmart. They have a series of software programs that can be tailor-made to suit various network marketing companies and their support systems. This is an excellent business tool that allows you to track and monitor the new people in your organisation while also enabling you to assess where existing people are at in terms of their volume and activity. It is also a great tool for goal-setting. If your network marketing company or support system is not familiar with WorXSmart it might be worthwhile promoting it to them. For further information, visit www.worxsmart.com.

# #118 Structure your business to be profitable

Building a profitable network marketing business is not just about throwing a bunch of people into a network and hoping that they buy or sell some product. More than likely, the company you are affiliated with will have a suggested structure to follow that is designed to make your business profitable.

This structure may be based on the number of people you sponsor personally, the number of people in your down-line, or the volume spread across your organisation. The important thing is that you make yourself aware of what that structure is. You may spend the same amount of time putting the same number of people into your organisation, but the difference will be that the time you have spent was creating a profitable business, rather than a not-so-profitable one.

If you were operating a traditional business you would need to understand what made it profitable and what did not. The same applies to your network marketing business. It is vital that as you build your network you continually assess how your team is coming together and where you need to focus your efforts to ensure that the time you invest will give you the best return.

# #119 Give and you will receive

Because your success is based on the principle of helping other people within your network become successful, the great universal law of 'give and you will receive' is certainly true of successful network marketing.

As you develop your team, try to adopt a mindset of taking your eyes off yourself and focusing on helping the people within your team. Learn what it is that your people want to achieve by being involved, then give your time and energy to helping them achieve their dreams. Help enough people in your team and you will receive whatever it is you are wishing to achieve by default.

## #120  Quitters never win and winners never quit

There are not many guarantees in life but one that comes close, particularly in network marketing, is 'if you quit you are not going to win'. To win means different things to different people; to you it may mean building a global network that represents millions of dollars of turnover and an ongoing active involvement; it may mean building the business to a certain level, whether that be large or small, then taking a back seat and not being so active in it; it may mean building the business to a certain pre-set level and moving on to do something else. Whatever the goal, one thing is certain: no one will ever reach it if they quit along the way.

The world is full of 'wannabes'. Most of them are quitters who never stick at something long enough to see it through. One of the greatest secrets to success is simply that 'if you don't quit, you will make it'. The time it takes to reach the goal will vary, but if you keep going it will happen.

Whatever the goal you have set yourself, make the decision that you are not going to quit, no matter what. Don't dwell on the time it takes, don't judge your performance on others around you, run your own race and . . . if you don't quit you will make it!

# #121 In the end, 'if it has to be, it's up to me'

It's an unfortunate fact that it has become all too common for people to blame others for their lot in life, or to feel that it's someone else's responsibility to help them to be successful. The reality is that it's up to *you* to choose the thoughts and actions that will lead you to success. Your life will be what you make of it. Nothing will ever happen by itself. Success will come your way once you realise that you have to make it yourself through your own actions.

The day you take complete responsibility for yourself, the day you stop making excuses, is the day you start moving forward on the road to success. No one else can do it for you. Only you can make it happen.

Network marketing is a great opportunity to create success in your life. Although there are strong support mechanisms in place and proven systems to follow, in the end it's up to you to make it happen.

# Notes on building a successful network marketing business

..........................................................................

..........................................................................

..........................................................................

..........................................................................

..........................................................................

..........................................................................

..........................................................................

..........................................................................

..........................................................................

..........................................................................

..........................................................................

..........................................................................

..........................................................................

..........................................................................

..........................................................................

..........................................................................

..........................................................................

..........................................................................

..........................................................................

..........................................................................

*Never, never, never, never . . . give in.*
**Winston Churchill**

# Thirty ongoing checks and balances

The following checklist will help you monitor whether you are on track. Using a pencil, circle the appropriate response at this time. Update this checklist monthly. Be honest with your answers. Use it when you are talking with your coach to identify any areas you might need help with. There are extra lines at the bottom to add items not included here that are relevant to you.

1  I have a good understanding of how my business works.

    YES          NEEDS IMPROVEMENT         NO

2  I have a good understanding of how best to structure my business to be profitable.

    YES          NEEDS IMPROVEMENT         NO

3  I have a written list of my dreams and I review it weekly.

    YES          NEEDS IMPROVEMENT         NO

4 I regularly go dream-building and take the opportunity to see and feel my dreams.

YES             NEEDS IMPROVEMENT             NO


5 I am firmly plugged into the support system provided.

YES             NEEDS IMPROVEMENT             NO


6 I am informed about and regularly access the tools available to me through the support system.

YES             NEEDS IMPROVEMENT             NO


7 I am a good promoter of tools to my team and I don't dilute the system.

YES             NEEDS IMPROVEMENT             NO


8 I read from a positive mental affirmation book for at least fifteen minutes per day.

YES             NEEDS IMPROVEMENT             NO


9 I listen to a positive mental affirmation tape or CD at least every week.

YES             NEEDS IMPROVEMENT             NO

10  I attend all meetings and functions promoted to me by my organisation.

   YES               NEEDS IMPROVEMENT                    NO

11  I am constantly striving to improve my people skills.

   YES               NEEDS IMPROVEMENT                    NO

12  I am confident and comfortable in providing leadership to my team.

   YES               NEEDS IMPROVEMENT                    NO

13  I am a 100 per cent user of the products available through my business.

   YES               NEEDS IMPROVEMENT                    NO

14  I have good knowledge of the products available through my network.

   YES               NEEDS IMPROVEMENT                    NO

15  I am comfortable in selling products.

   YES               NEEDS IMPROVEMENT                    NO

16  I am constantly adding new people to my prospect list.

   YES               NEEDS IMPROVEMENT                    NO

17  I am confident in contacting people to look at my business.

YES                 NEEDS IMPROVEMENT                  NO


18  I am presenting the business idea to people on a regular basis in line with a recommended number promoted by my organisation.

YES                 NEEDS IMPROVEMENT                  NO


19  My conversion rate of sponsoring people to presentations made is good.

YES                 NEEDS IMPROVEMENT                  NO


20  I am good at overcoming objections.

YES                 NEEDS IMPROVEMENT                  NO


21  I am good at leading people when they are getting started.

YES                 NEEDS IMPROVEMENT                  NO


22  I have developed a relationship with a company representative from within the network marketing company I am affiliated with.

YES                 NEEDS IMPROVEMENT                  NO


23  I freely look for advice and guidance from the leaders above me in my organisation.

YES                 NEEDS IMPROVEMENT                  NO

24  I regularly meet with my coach to discuss my goals and challenges.

YES                 NEEDS IMPROVEMENT                 NO

25  I am happy with my levels of health and fitness.

YES                 NEEDS IMPROVEMENT                 NO

26  I am happy with the relationships I have with family and friends.

YES                 NEEDS IMPROVEMENT                 NO

27  I am not letting my previous failures or baggage hold me back.

YES                 NEEDS IMPROVEMENT                 NO

28  I am constantly updating myself on who the new people are in my team and who are my key players.

YES                 NEEDS IMPROVEMENT                 NO

29  I am consistent and persistent in building my business.

YES                 NEEDS IMPROVEMENT                 NO

30  My attitude is better than anyone else's in my team. I am positive and uplifting to be around.

YES                 NEEDS IMPROVEMENT                 NO

**Additional topics:**

. . . . . . . . . . . . . . . . . . . . . . . . . . . . . . . . . . . . . . . . . . . . . . . . . . . . . . . . . . . . . . . .

YES                    NEEDS IMPROVEMENT                    NO

. . . . . . . . . . . . . . . . . . . . . . . . . . . . . . . . . . . . . . . . . . . . . . . . . . . . . . . . . . . . . . . .

YES                    NEEDS IMPROVEMENT                    NO

. . . . . . . . . . . . . . . . . . . . . . . . . . . . . . . . . . . . . . . . . . . . . . . . . . . . . . . . . . . . . . . .

YES                    NEEDS IMPROVEMENT                    NO

. . . . . . . . . . . . . . . . . . . . . . . . . . . . . . . . . . . . . . . . . . . . . . . . . . . . . . . . . . . . . . . .

YES                    NEEDS IMPROVEMENT                    NO

. . . . . . . . . . . . . . . . . . . . . . . . . . . . . . . . . . . . . . . . . . . . . . . . . . . . . . . . . . . . . . . .

YES                    NEEDS IMPROVEMENT                    NO

. . . . . . . . . . . . . . . . . . . . . . . . . . . . . . . . . . . . . . . . . . . . . . . . . . . . . . . . . . . . . . . .

YES                    NEEDS IMPROVEMENT                    NO

. . . . . . . . . . . . . . . . . . . . . . . . . . . . . . . . . . . . . . . . . . . . . . . . . . . . . . . . . . . . . . . .

YES                    NEEDS IMPROVEMENT                    NO

# Final note from the authors

If you run your network marketing business on sound, sustainable and realistic business practices you will be well on the way to success. No one knows how to do all of this naturally, so don't be too hard on yourself. It is like going back to school. Having a thirst for the knowledge that will help you to succeed is the first step. Talk to other people in your business, talk to mainstream business people, have goals, be persistent and be disciplined—and most importantly of all, have so much fun that you almost burst.

*Andrew Griffiths*

Having your own business provides an opportunity to be in control of your own destiny. Many people will never be given that opportunity; don't let your chance slip by. It's been said that the average person only gets three genuine opportunities during the course of their lives. What number are you up to?

Your journey along the way in building your network marketing business will be a combination of highs and lows, peaks and troughs, victories and failures. Most of all it will be a series of discoveries, about yourself and about others. Embrace the opportunity to grow personally as well as financially.

To make a success of any business venture will be about perseverance and having a good attitude more than anything else. It is not letting the setbacks get you down and, most importantly, it is maintaining a 'never give up' attitude.

Try to remember that your network marketing business is simply a vehicle and like all vehicles it won't go anywhere without fuel in the tank. Your dream is that fuel. Next, you must have someone to drive the vehicle, otherwise it will just sit there and do nothing. You are that driver. And finally, unless you have a destination and are clear on how to get there, you will drive around aimlessly until you run out of fuel.

Treat your network marketing business as just that, a business. Give it the respect and commitment needed with any business and then give it all you've got.

I wish you all the success for the future. Follow your dreams—you can do it, I believe in you!

*Wayne Toms*

# Recommended reading

Blanchard, K. and Johnson, S., 1981 *The One Minute Manager*, William Morrow, New York

Bruber, M.W., 1995 *The E Myth Revisited*, HarperCollins, New York

Cairo, J., 1998 *Motivation and Goal-Setting*, Career Press

Canfield, J., 2007 *How to Get From Where You Are to Where You Want to be*, Harper Element, London

Carnegie, D., [1936] 1981 *How to Win Friends and Influence People*, HarperCollins, New York

Covey, S., 1990 *The 7 Habits of Highly Effective People*, Simon & Schuster, New York

Dodd, P. and Sundheim, D., 2005 *25 Best Time Management Tools and Techniques*, self-published

Godin, S., 2003 *Purple Cow*, Penguin Group, New York

Hill, N., 1979 *Success Through a Positive Mental Attitude*, Pocket Books, New York

Keller, J. 1999 *Attitude is Everything*, International Training Institute, Tampa

Kiyosaki, R., 2001 *The Business School—For People Who Like Helping People*, Cashflow Technologies Inc., Arizona

Kiyosaki, R. and Lechter, S., 2000 *Cashflow Quadrant*, Hachette, New York

Littauer, F., 1993 *Personality Plus*, Fleming H. Revell, Michigan

Maxwell, J., 1998 *The 21 Irrefutable Laws of Leadership*, Thomas Nelson, Nashville

McGrath, J., 2003 *You Inc*, HarperCollins, Sydney

Morgenstern, J., 2000 *Time Management from the Inside Out*, Henry Holt and Company, New York

Rohm, R.A., 1999 *Sponsor with Style*, Insight International Inc., Atlanta

Rouillard, L.A., 2002 *Goals and Goal-Setting*, Thompson Crisp Learning

Schwartz, D., 1987 *The Magic of Thinking Big*, Simon & Schuster, New York

# About the authors

## Andrew Griffiths

Andrew Griffiths is an entrepreneur with a passion for small business. From humble beginnings as an orphan growing up in Western Australia, Andrew has owned and operated a number of successful small businesses, with his first enterprise—at age seven—being a paper round. Since then, he has sold encyclopaedias door to door, travelled the world as an international sales manager, worked in the Great Sandy Desert for a gold exploration company and been a commercial diver. Clearly this unusual combination of experiences has made him the remarkable man he is.

Inspired by his constant desire to see others reach their goals, Andrew has written seven hugely successful books, with many more on the way. His *101 Ways* series offers small business owners practical, passionate and achievable advice. The series is sold in over 40 countries worldwide.

Andrew is the founding director of **The Oceanic Marketing Group**, one of Australia's best and most respected strategic marketing and corporate imaging firms.

Known for his ability to entertain, inspire and deliver key messages, Andrew is also a powerful keynote presenter, who brings flamboyant energy and verve to the corporate world. All of this occurs from his chosen home of Cairns, North Queensland, Great Barrier Reef, Australia.

To find out more about Andrew Griffiths please visit the following websites:
www.andrewgriffiths.com.au
www.oceanicmarketinggroup.com.au
www.enhanceplus.com.au
www.allenandunwin.com

## Wayne Toms

Wayne is a successful entrepreneur based in New South Wales, Australia. Married with three children, he has a background in management, traditional business and investing. Recognising the opportunity to leverage and duplicate yourself that network marketing provides, and to create passive income, Wayne, along with his wife, Colleen, entered into network marketing in 1991. Since that time they have created a successful network marketing business and are recognised and also highly regarded within the industry for their leadership and teaching abilities.

Today their network marketing business provides them with ongoing passive income and other non-cash rewards. The income from their network marketing business has provided them with additional cashflow which has been used to foster lifestyle and fund wealth creation through investments, property and the establishment of other business ventures.

They are currently taking time off from actively building their network marketing business while developing Enhance Plus, a company they established three years ago, which is in the stages of being franchised both nationally and internationally. The principles behind this business venture were born out of their involvement in network marketing.

For more information on Enhance Plus visit:
www.enhanceplus.com.au
For more information on Wayne Toms visit:
www.waynetoms.com

## 101 WAYS TO MARKET YOUR BUSINESS

**Stand out from the crowd.**

Here are 101 practical marketing suggestions to help you achieve dramatic improvements in your business without investing a lot of time and money.

Simple, affordable and quick, these innovative tips are easy to implement and will bring you fast results. Choose and apply at least one new idea each week or use this book as a source of inspiration for new ways to market your services, your products and your business itself.

With tips that take just a few moments to read, *101 Ways to Market Your Business* will help you find new customers, increase the loyalty of the customers you already have, create great promotional material and make your business stand out from the crowd.

INCLUDES 20 BONUS SUGGESTIONS TO HELP YOU ATTRACT NEW CUSTOMERS AND KEEP YOUR EXISTING ONES

## 101 WAYS TO ADVERTISE YOUR BUSINESS

**Read this before you spend another cent on advertising.**

Here are 101 proven tips to increase the effectiveness of your advertising. Use these tips to understand what makes one ad work while another fails and you will save a small fortune in wasted advertising.

With tips that take just a few moments to read, *101 Ways to Advertise Your Business* offers step-by-step advice on how to make an advertisement, how to buy advertising space and how to ensure that your advertisement is working to its full potential. Follow the tips and your business will soon be reaping the benefits.

INCLUDES A SPECIAL BONUS SECTION CONTAINING HUNDREDS OF THE BEST ADVERTISING WORDS AND PHRASES

## 101 WAYS TO REALLY SATISFY YOUR CUSTOMERS

**Simple ways to keep your customers coming back.**

Here are 101 practical tips for delivering service that exceeds your customers' expectations and keeps them coming back. In a world where consumers are far more informed, discerning and demanding than ever before, customer service is one of the main areas where a business can outshine its competitors.

Use these simple tips to improve your customer service and you will be well on the way to success and profitability. With tips that take just a few moments to read, *101 Ways to Really Satisfy Your Customers* teaches you to identify what customers expect, and details simple suggestions that will enable your business to exceed these expectations and reap the rewards.

INCLUDES 20 BONUS TIPS THAT WILL REALLY IMPRESS YOUR CUSTOMERS

## 101 WAYS TO BOOST YOUR BUSINESS

**Energise your business today!**

Here are 101 powerful tips to kick-start your business and unlock some of the potential that may be struggling to break through.

With tips that take just a few moments to read, *101 Ways to Boost Your Business* shows you how to make your business better and ultimately more profitable. These no-nonsense tips can be actioned immediately, so you will see results quickly.

These tips cover a host of everyday business issues, and are equally applicable to all industries in each and every corner of the world. They will save you thousands of dollars.

INCLUDES 20 BONUS TIPS THAT WILL RECHARGE YOUR BUSINESS

## 101 WAYS TO HAVE A BUSINESS AND A LIFE

**Put the passion back into your business and your life**

Is your business all-consuming? Are you tired of feeling over-whelmed every day? Would you like to take control of your life again?

If, like most business owners, you are struggling to balance your business and your life, don't worry! *101 Ways to Have a Business and a Life* provides simple, practical ideas that will help you to identify the reasons behind this lack of balance and what to do about it. Andrew Griffiths has consulted thousands of business owners around the world and compiled their experiences and coping mechanisms into one easy reference book. All of the tips can be implemented quickly and at little or no cost. You can be the boss of your business and your life.

INCLUDES 20 BONUS SUGGESTIONS TO ENSURE THAT YOU'RE THE ONE CALLING THE SHOTS IN YOUR BUSINESS WORLD